The Cambridge Introduction to
Walt Whitman

Walt Whitman is one of the most innovative and influential American
poets of the nineteenth century. Focusing on his masterpiece *Leaves of
Grass*, this book provides a foundation for the study of Whitman as an
experimental poet, a radical democrat, and a historical personality in the
era of the American Civil War, the growth of the great cities, and the
westward expansion of the United States. Always a controversial and
important figure, Whitman continues to attract the admiration of poets,
artists, critics, political activists, and readers around the world. Those
studying his work for the first time will find this an invaluable book.
Alongside close readings of the major texts, chapters on Whitman's
biography, the history and culture of his time, and the critical reception
of his work provide a comprehensive understanding of Whitman and of
how he has become such a central figure in the American literary canon.

M. Jimmie Killingsworth is Professor of English at Texas A&M
University. He has published widely on Whitman and on nineteenth-
century American literature.

Cambridge Introductions to Literature

This series is designed to introduce students to key topics and authors. Accessible and lively, these introductions will also appeal to readers who want to broaden their understanding of the books and authors they enjoy.

- Ideal for students, teachers, and lecturers
- Concise, yet packed with essential information
- Key suggestions for further reading

Titles in this series

The Cambridge Introduction to
Walt Whitman

M. JIMMIE KILLINGSWORTH

CAMBRIDGE
UNIVERSITY PRESS

CAMBRIDGE UNIVERSITY PRESS
Cambridge, New York, Melbourne, Madrid, Cape Town, Singapore, São Paulo

Cambridge University Press
The Edinburgh Building, Cambridge CB2 2RU, UK

Published in the United States of America by Cambridge University Press, New York

www.cambridge.org
Information on this title: www.cambridge.org/9780521670944

First published 2007

Printed in the United Kingdom at the University Press, Cambridge

A catalogue record for this publication is available from the British Library

Library of Congress Cataloguing in Publication data
Killingsworth, M. Jimmie.
The Cambridge introduction to Walt Whitman / M. Jimmie Killingsworth.
    p.   cm.
Includes bibliographical references and index.
ISBN-13: 978-0-521-85456-6 (hardback)
ISBN-10: 0-521-85456-3 (hardback)
ISBN-13: 978-0-521-67094-4 (pbk.)
ISBN-10: 0-521-67094-2 (pbk.)
1. Whitman, Walt, 1819–1892 – Handbooks, manuals, etc.   2. Poets, American –
19th century – Biography – Handbooks, manuals, etc.   I. Title.

PS3231. K55   2007
811'. 3 – dc22   2006031964

ISBN 978-0-521-85456-6 hardback
ISBN 978-0-521-67094-4 paperback

Contents

Preface

Walt Whitman (1819–92) is generally regarded as one of the two most innovative and influential US poets of the nineteenth century (the other is Emily Dickinson). A powerful voice for democracy, a bold innovator in verse form, the controversial "poet of the body," and the consummate individualist who dared to proclaim "I celebrate myself," Whitman continues to attract the admiration of poets, artists, critics, mystics, political activists, and adventurous readers around the world.

This book serves as an introductory guide for students and first-time readers of Whitman. It covers the style and ideas of the poetry (Chapters 3 and 4) as well as the major prose writings (Chapter 5). It also contextualizes Whitman's writing and thought with short chapters on biography (Chapter 1), history and culture (Chapter 2), and the critical reception of the work from its first publication to the present (Chapter 6). The book is designed to be read from start to finish for readers needing a fast overview, but the various parts stand more or less on their own. The one exception to this general rule is that readers primarily interested in the study of individual poems should first read the treatment of "Song of Myself" in Chapter 3 to gain an understanding of Whitman's most important themes and experiments in poetic form. Readings of other poems tend to refer back to this foundational treatment.

To promote readability, citations of secondary critical and biographical works are kept to a minimum and critical controversies are sometimes simplified. A select annotated bibliography, limited mainly to books still in print, is provided for the reader who wishes to take the next step in Whitman studies. In the interest of simplifying references to the many editions and versions of Whitman's writings, citations in the discussions of Whitman's works in all chapters refer as much as possible to a single source, selected for its range, dependability, and accessibility. This is the Library of America edition of Whitman's *Complete Poetry and Collected Prose* (1982). Unless otherwise indicated, parenthetical references cite this edition by page number. Although I will be treating the poems in their order of original publication, beginning with those dating from 1855, I will be using the best-known titles and texts of the poems, the ones that appeared in the 1891–2 Deathbed Edition of *Leaves of Grass*, largely because these are the titles and texts most available to current readers. Readers interested in the changes Whitman made in each edition – which are considerable and which have stimulated some excellent work in bibliography and textual criticism – should consult the online *Walt Whitman Archive* edited by Ed Folsom and Kenneth M. Price, an essential resource in Whitman studies.

I wish to thank Ray Ryan and the staff at Cambridge University Press for inviting me to contribute to this series of literary introductions and for all their help in producing the book. I am also grateful to those who have read the manuscript and offered valuable suggestions, notably Pete Messent (for the Press), Nicole DuPlessis, Steve Marsden, and my distinguished colleague at Texas A&M University, Jerome Loving. Thanks also go to my wife and frequent co-author Jacqueline Palmer and my daughter Myrth Killingsworth for their editorial help and to Myrth's friends at Rice University, Birte Wehmeier and Matilda Young, who served as trial readers early in the project.

Chapter 1

Life

The central event of Walt Whitman's life, literally and figuratively, was the publication of *Leaves of Grass*. The first edition appeared in 1855, when the poet was thirty-six years old. For the rest of his life, roughly thirty-six more years, he would revise and expand the book through six more editions, his work culminating in the Deathbed Edition of 1891–92. Whitman identified himself completely with *Leaves of Grass*. In the poem "So Long" at the end of the third (1860) edition, he says, "this is no book / Who touches this touches a man."[1]

Whitman also identified strongly with US history and the American people. What Whitman called his "language experiment" paralleled the experiment of democracy in the new world, as he saw it.[2] His book appeared first in the troubled years leading up to the Civil War. When war erupted in 1861, his life and his work were deeply altered.

This chapter focuses on the close connection between Whitman's life and his writings. In briefly acknowledging the currents of history that touched Whitman most directly – the momentous effects of modernization in everything from the mass media and democratic politics to gender roles and war – it anticipates Chapter 2, which covers the main historical contexts. The chapter is divided into four parts: youth and literary apprenticeship (1819–50), the emergence of the poet (1851–60), the Civil War and its aftermath (1861–73), and the period of reflection and decline (1873–92). Each part is keyed to different stages in Whitman's literary work and marked by shifts of emphasis in his poetic theories and practices occasioned by personal and historical change.

1

Youth and literary apprenticeship (1819–1850)

The poet was born Walter Whitman, Jr., on 31 May 1819 in West Hills, Long Island, New York, the second son of Walter and Louisa Van Velsor Whitman. He was four years old when his father, a carpenter, moved the family from the house he had built himself in the village of West Hills to the thriving town of Brooklyn, where he had built a new house. During Whitman's early life, the elder Whitman often shuffled the family from house to house, selling one and occupying another as new houses were built. They moved frequently, alternating between town and country on Long Island.

Patriotism ran high in the Whitman family. Whitman's father was an avid reader who passed on to his son the most radical heritage of Revolutionary-era freethinking and democratic politics. As a sign of his patriotism, he named the sons born after young Walter, in succession, Andrew Jackson, George Washington, and Thomas Jefferson Whitman. His mother spiritualized the heritage, introducing Whitman to the practices and doctrines of American Quakerism. In 1829, the family went to hear the famous Quaker preacher Elias Hicks, whose charisma and vocal power Whitman never forgot.

The reading and exposure to intellectual life at home were all the more important because Whitman had little chance for formal education as a boy from a working-class family. He attended school only until about 1830, at which time he went to work and continued an informal education in the circulating library, the printing offices, the public lecture halls, and the debating societies of Long Island.

As a teenager in 1835, unable to count on support from his parents who were struggling to take care of an expanding family (six sons and a daughter, all but one younger than the future poet), he signed on as an apprentice printer in Manhattan. A fire destroyed the heart of New York's printing industry before he could find regular work, but he later used his skills as a printer to work his way into the field of journalism.

Back on Long Island in 1836, Whitman tried his hand at schoolteaching, living with his family or boarding at homes of students. The work left him frustrated and disillusioned. Exposure to big-city life had given him ambitions and attitudes that made him resent the job and feel superior to his rural neighbors. Of one teaching post, he wrote in an 1840 letter, "O, damnation, damnation! thy other name is school-teaching and thy residence Woodbury."[3] But Whitman's interest in public education stayed with him well after he gave up teaching. He editorialized on the topic during his newspaper years in the 1840s and kept the pedagogical spirit alive in his greatest poems. "Have you practic'd so long to learn to read?" he asks in "Song of Myself": "Stop this day and night with me and you shall possess the origin of all poems" (189).

Journalism provided some relief from the boredom of teaching and country life. In 1838, he started his own paper, *The Long Islander*, doing all the printing and writing himself. Other papers occasionally reprinted his articles, as well as his first published poem, "Our Future Lot." His paper lasted less than a year, but it led to employment at other papers and to more publications, including the prose series "The Sun-Down Papers," perhaps the first indication of real literary talent in the young Whitman. He wrote and published short stories based on home life and teaching as well as more poems on conventional themes – sentimental treatments of love and death, for example – and on people and events in the news. He would return to writing poems about the news again during the Civil War, and would continue the practice to the end of his life.

The 1840s proved an important decade in Whitman's literary apprenticeship. Beginning in 1841 with a job at the *New World*, he was finally able to support himself primarily as a journalist. In 1842, he became editor of the *Aurora*, a prominent New York daily. He wrote regularly on local politics, literature, education, and entertainment while continuing to contribute to other periodicals. Living in Manhattan boarding houses and immersing himself in the life of the city, he heard lectures or readings by famous authors, including Dickens and Emerson, and developed an interest in theatre and music, particularly opera, which strongly influenced his mature poetry. Increasingly, he caught the attention of important people on the literary scene. He wrote short stories that appeared in such venues as the *United States Magazine and Democratic Review*, which also published works by Bryant, Whittier, Longfellow, and Hawthorne, some of the most successful authors of the day.

Scholars have traditionally viewed the early fiction as sensationalistic and conventional, though in recent years critics have reassessed the stories, working through the undistinguished style and haze of sentimentality to discover social and psychological themes that would grow to greater significance in *Leaves of Grass*. His favorite topics included sympathy for the common people, the difficulties of childhood and adolescence, family dysfunction, the relations of classes in the emerging democracy, the joys and evils of city life, and above all, the sensual intensity of men thrown together in unfamiliar urban settings. The themes converge in *Franklin Evans, or the Inebriate*, a temperance novel Whitman published in 1842 on the evils of drinking. Though it sold surprisingly well, Whitman later treated his accomplishment dismissively and debunked the temperance movement. He told Horace Traubel that he wrote the novel only for the money, in a fever of productivity fueled by alcohol.[4]

Politics also played a big part in Whitman's life in the 1840s. A speech he gave at a Democratic rally not long after he first arrived in Manhattan was praised in the *Evening Post*, edited by William Cullen Bryant. As a young journalist, his support of the Democrats probably paved the way for some jobs and lost him others in the highly partisan world of the newspapers. The Party was divided between liberals, to whom the independent Whitman was usually drawn, especially in his opposition to slavery, and the conservative wing, which was centered in the south. In 1846, as editor of the Brooklyn *Daily Eagle*, the most important paper in his fast-growing hometown, Whitman intensified his political commitments, writing editorials supporting the Mexican War and objecting to the expansion of slavery into the west.

He had the chance to witness the buying and selling of slaves first-hand in February 1848, when he traveled to New Orleans with his younger brother Thomas Jefferson (Jeff) to take a new job at a New Orleans paper, the *Crescent*. He lasted only three months, driven home by Jeff's homesickness and his own disagreements with the newspaper management. But the opportunity to travel across the country and down the Mississippi and to see a city very different from New York gave Whitman the perspective he needed both to appreciate his home region and to imagine himself reaching out to become the bard of a broad and varied land. The cosmopolitan setting and Old World feel of New Orleans may have contributed to Whitman's newfound interest in transatlantic affairs. The European Revolutions of 1848 caught his attention and encouraged his hope for a worldwide democracy that would look to America as a model. Whitman reflects on the 1848 revolutions in a poem first published in the New York *Tribune* in 1850. Later known by the title "Europe, the 72d and 73d Years of These States," it would become one of two previously published political poems to be included with the poetry written expressly for the 1855 *Leaves of Grass*. The other was "A Boston Ballad," which recounts the arrest and trial of a fugitive slave in 1854.

On his return to Brooklyn, Whitman joined the new Free-Soil Party, devoted to keeping the land west of the Mississippi free of slavery. In the Fall of 1848, he was elected as a delegate to the convention in Buffalo to nominate a candidate for President and became editor of a Party paper, the *Brooklyn Weekly Freeman*. With the defeat of the Free-Soil candidate, Martin Van Buren, by the Whig candidate Zachary Taylor, enthusiasm waned, and some party members made their peace with the Democrats. When Whitman resigned from the *Freeman* in September 1849, the paper folded. In 1850, he wrote two poems expressing his bitterness over the politics of compromise. "Blood Money," published in the New York *Tribune Supplement*, compared Massachusetts senator Daniel Webster to Judas Iscariot because of his support for the Fugitive Slave Law, which imposed fines on federal marshals who failed to arrest runaway slaves and on people who aided the fugitives in free states. "The House of Friends," also published in the *Tribune*, voiced the poet's disappointment and frustration over the Compromise of 1850, which expanded the legality of slavery westward.

The emergence of the poet (1851–1860)

In the early 1850s, Whitman withdrew somewhat from the public life that had bitterly disappointed him. He worked off and on as a carpenter with his father. For a while, he ran a bookstore out of his home. And he filled notebook after notebook with a new kind of poetry. With the death of his father coinciding almost exactly with the publication of the first edition of *Leaves of Grass* in 1855, he used the occasion to redefine himself as a man, a poet, and a subject of poetry – "Walt Whitman, an American, a kosmos, one of the roughs," as he named himself in the 1855 version of "Song of Myself," leaving aside the "Walter" by which he had been known in all his previous writings and coming before the public as a more urgent and intimate voice (50).

It was on Independence Day, 4 July 1855 (at least according to the poet's own, probably mythic, dating) that Whitman issued the first edition of *Leaves of Grass*. The book was a thin green oversized volume with twelve untitled poems – including some that would one day be counted among his most famous, such as "Song of Myself," "The Sleepers," and "I Sing the Body Electric," as they would later be titled – and a ten-page preface on poetic and political principles that was itself something of a prose poem. Whitman not only wrote the book but set some of the type and served as his own publisher.

His career in journalism set him up for the publication, as even the name of the book reveals. "Grass" was a slang term among printers for throw-away print samples that they wrote themselves. "Leaves" referred to pages, of course, but also to bundles of paper.[5] In addition, the title alluded to the Bible, which Whitman had read attentively from his earliest youth. The prophet Isaiah says, "All flesh is grass, and all its beauty is like the flower of the field. The grass withereth, the flower fadeth, because the breath of the Lord bloweth upon it; surely the people are grass" (Isaiah 40.6). For the poet-prophet Whitman, the beauty of the body – the very fleshiness of human life in its most common experience – was the root experience of democracy and humanity en masse. In proclaiming himself the poet of the body as well as the poet of the soul, Whitman set out to celebrate the material body and the common people, the "grass" that previous poets had neglected.

Whitman used his connections in journalism not only to print but also to promote his book. He placed anonymous self-reviews of *Leaves of Grass* in three New York periodicals. In the *United States Review*, he announced "An American bard at last!" In the Brooklyn *Daily Eagle*, he praised the artistic originality of this hometown poet whose writing "conforms to none of the rules by which poetry has ever been judged." And in the *American Phrenological Journal*, he welcomed a poetry for the common people and declared American literature's independence from the English, whose poetry, for all its greatness, still emitted an "air which to America is the air of death."[6]

The book did not sell many copies, but the efforts of Whitman and the publishing firm of Fowler and Wells, which agreed to serve as his main distributor, did make an impression on the literary scene. Critical responses in the press (excluding Whitman's own) ranged from utter indignation to mild appreciation (see Chapter 6). The most important response – and perhaps the most famous encounter of one writer with another in American literary history – came not in a public review but in a private letter from Ralph Waldo Emerson, the renowned philosopher, poet, and essayist, to whom Whitman had boldly sent a personal copy. Emerson responded to the relatively unknown writer almost immediately and with great enthusiasm in a letter on 21 July 1855: "I find [your book] the most extraordinary piece of wit & wisdom that America has yet contributed. I am very happy in reading it, as great power makes us happy."[7]

This encouragement from Emerson in literary Boston, as well as the support of Fowler and Wells in New York, sent Whitman into a fever of composition. By 1856 he had greatly expanded the number of poems and was ready to bring out a new edition. The second edition of *Leaves* was a compact, pocket-sized book of poems – all including the word "poem" in their titles, lest anyone try to second-guess his intention to create a new kind of poetry in free verse and not just oddly lineated prose. The formerly untitled works now appeared under such titles as "Poem of Walt Whitman, an American" (later "Song of Myself") and "Poem of the Body" ("I Sing the Body Electric"). The new poems included some of the most infamous, such as "Poem of Procreation" ("A Woman Waits for Me"), which augmented Whitman's poetry of the body, perhaps under the influence of Fowler and Wells, who were themselves the authors and publishers of faddish books on health and human reproduction. Among the most inspired works in the new book was "Sun-Down Poem," later titled "Crossing Brooklyn Ferry." The 1855 Preface was gone, but at the end of the book, Whitman printed, without permission, the complete text of Emerson's letter and a long response of his own, which began "Dear Master" and lectured at length on his poetic theories and ambitions. If that was not enough, Whitman had the opening words of Emerson's letter printed on the book's spine – "I greet you at the beginning of a great career. – R. W. Emerson" – and thus introduced the practice of using promotional "blurbs" into American literary history. Not surprisingly, Emerson took offense and cooled somewhat toward Whitman. Even so, he generously continued to support the younger poet with advice and encouragement throughout his career.

Whitman's poetic ambitions continued to expand. In 1857, he projected a new volume of his poems. In one note, he referred to this work in progress as "the Great Construction of the New Bible."[8] But poetry was not paying the bills, so he continued to work at journalism. By this time, however, he was no longer driven by journalistic ambition or political interest but by economic necessity. His self-image now centered on his role as the poet of democracy.

Whitman also may have begun to question his own sexual identity. Some biographers have suggested that he experienced a deep and disturbing love affair with another man in the late 1850s. One name frequently mentioned in this connection is Fred Vaughan, an omnibus driver whom Whitman certainly befriended. Though the evidence for this particular connection is weak, there is little doubt that Whitman worried over his erotic attraction to other men. He produced a manuscript of intensely emotional poems, a kind of sonnet sequence he called "Live Oak, with Moss," which he never published as such but developed into the first group of poems arranged as a "cluster" in *Leaves of Grass*, the "Calamus" poems of the third edition. These poems preserve a fascinating tension between celebration of the joy of same-sex friendship and anxiety over the fear of loss and the nature of the erotic bond. The psychological darkness offers a new complexity to the 1860 *Leaves*.

The expanded edition, which swelled to 456 pages, adding 146 new poems to the 32 of 1856, continued to celebrate America with hope and energy. Whitman's commitment to the poetry of the body and the physical foundation of human attraction remained intact, especially in the two new clusters of poems – the "Calamus" poems on the love of comrades and "Enfans d'Adam" (later "Children of Adam") on the attraction of man to woman. But the new book also had its special character and differences. Above all the darker emotions that colored some of the "Calamus" poems also appeared elsewhere, most notably in the poems ultimately known as "Out of the Cradle Endlessly Rocking," Whitman's great poem of spiritual autobiography, and the melancholy "As I Ebb'd with the Ocean of Life." The ebb-tide tone of the new poems – in contrast to the optimistic energy of 1855 and such 1856 poems as "Crossing Brooklyn Ferry," which celebrates the flood-tide ecstasy of a deathless life – suggests that Whitman experienced serious doubt and depression during these years, in which he questioned his vocation as the poet of democracy and all but abandoned his mission. He had no steady employment and felt increasing responsibility to provide money and emotional support for his widowed mother who was keeping house for siblings beset with mental illness, debilitation, marital troubles, alcoholism, and disease.

Things only got worse when it became time to publish the book. In Thayer and Eldridge of Boston, Whitman had found a young publishing firm with great enthusiasm for his poetry. The publishers sought him out in New York, signed a contract, allowed Whitman the freedom to influence the details of publication, and energetically promoted the new *Leaves of Grass*. But the book had barely been released when, in 1861, war erupted. Like many companies, Thayer and Eldridge were thrown into bankruptcy.

The war and its aftermath (1861–1873)

Whitman came to view the Civil War as the spiritual and moral center of his life and work. When the war began, he first responded with "recruitment poems," such as "Beat! Beat! Drums!" published in September 1861 in *Harper's Weekly* and the New York *Leader*. But for most of the year 1862, he appeared at loose ends. He retreated to Long Island and seems to have worked at avoiding the reality of war. Many of his fellow New Yorkers questioned the way the conflict was being managed, especially after the bad beginning for the Union troops at Bull Run and other battles. Whitman may have had his own doubts.

It was family duty that finally brought him face to face with the war. On 16 December 1862, the New York *Herald* published a list of New York soldiers wounded at the tragic battle of Fredericksburg in Virginia. The list included the misspelled name of Whitman's brother George. Propelled into action, Whitman left that very day and, with the help of friends in Washington, made his way to the place the army was camped in Falmouth, Virginia. The grim reality of the war greeted him in a pile of amputated limbs he saw outside a surgeon's tent. But he found his brother safe, his wound already healing. George would go on to have a distinguished service record, which included serving time as prisoner of war.

On 29 December, Whitman wrote to tell his mother that George was well and that he had decided to seek employment in Washington and stay close to the war. On the same day, he wrote to Emerson, requesting letters of introduction to key figures associated with Abraham Lincoln's Republican administration, including the abolitionist Charles Sumner, one of the founders of the Party and one of the few senators who had voted against measures like the Fugitive Slave Act. With Emerson's letter and with the help of his former publisher

Charles Eldridge, as well as the support of the people who would become his most valuable friends in Washington, William Douglas O'Connor and his wife Ellen, Whitman was hired as a copyist in the Army Paymaster's office and made his home in Washington, where he would live for the next ten years.

Within days of moving to Washington, the poet realized his truest wartime vocation as he began to make visits to the wounded and dying in the war hospitals. Moved by the bravery and personal beauty of these young men, mostly uneducated boys from the farms and towns of America, Whitman became something of an institution in the hospitals. He brought refreshments for the soldiers, read the Bible to them or whatever else they requested, wrote letters home on their behalf (and wrote to them once they returned to the front or to home), stood by during some fearsome medical treatments, and sat many a death watch as gangrene or illness wore away at the unlucky ones. He felt no animosity toward the Confederate wounded, whom he treated the same as the Union soldiers. Once, upon seeing a group of the rebels marching to prison, he was stirred with compassion and called them, in his notebook, "brothers . . . Americans silent proud young fellows."[9] He solicited funds from friends, acquaintances, and well-known public people to support his work and used his own money as well. He became deeply involved with some of the soldiers, exchanged kisses and hugs with them, which most received gladly, and expressed his affection in letters. The hopes he had vented in "Calamus" for a society rooted in "the dear love of comrades" no doubt seemed well-founded to him in these conditions only one step removed from the battleground. And yet the hard reality of the war pressed in upon him and may have made his earlier life and writing seem frivolous. The war "was not a quadrille in a ball-room," he would eventually write (779); it was "about nine hundred and ninety nine parts diarrhea to one part glory."[10]

He poured himself into the hospital work, to the point that the friends he made among the military doctors began to worry about his health. At midyear in 1864, he had to return for a time to Brooklyn to recover from weakness and a bad sore throat. By the end of the war, he was a physical wreck. If the war "saved" him in a spiritual sense, it may have destroyed him physically.

Whitman dedicated his writing in those years to recounting the terrible power of the war. As early as 5 January 1863, he dispatched an article to the Brooklyn *Daily Eagle*, "Our Brooklyn Boys in the War," in praise of his brother's regiment. In February he published "The Great Army of the Sick: Military Hospitals in Washington" in the New York *Times*. He continued to produce articles for the New York papers throughout the national crisis. He later collected his Civil War journalism and unpublished prose reflections in *Memoranda During the War* (1875) and *Specimen Days and Collect* (1882) (see Chapter 5).

Whitman was writing new poems as well. Not long after his article on the Brooklyn regiment was published, he wrote to Emerson about his idea of producing a short book of poetry on the war. The idea grew into *Drum-Taps*, which was first published as an independent book in 1865, then expanded with a "Sequel" in 1866 after the assassination of Lincoln, and finally incorporated as a cluster in *Leaves of Grass. Drum-Taps* stands with Herman Melville's *Battle Pieces* as the best poetry the war produced. Whitman told William O'Connor, "I consider Drum Taps superior to *Leaves of Grass*," adding: "I probably mean as a work of art."[11] Largely composed of short poems marked by vivid imagery and the elegiac tone that Whitman had experimented with in 1860 but now found better suited to his subject matter, the book would also include the poem that many critics consider his crowning achievement, "When Lilacs Last in the Dooryard Bloom'd," an extended elegy on the death of Lincoln, as well as the more conventional "O Captain! My Captain!" – which would become Whitman's most popular poem in his own lifetime.

President Lincoln filled a special place not only in Whitman's poetry but also in his understanding of America. During the war, Whitman frequently saw Lincoln passing through the streets. He admired the rough-hewn look of the President, his western background, and his determination in the face of adversity. By the time Lincoln was assassinated just after the end of the war in April 1865, Whitman felt a special bond with him. "I love the president personally," he had written in his diary on 31 October 1863.[12] There is some slight evidence, taken as gospel truth by some biographers, that the feeling was mutual, that Lincoln read *Leaves of Grass* in his Springfield, Illinois, law offices and that he once remarked on seeing Whitman on the streets, "Well, *he* looks like a *man*."[13] The "Lilacs" elegy used the death of Lincoln to commemorate the sacrifice of all those who died in the war and to proclaim the need for the living to honor their memory by preserving the deepest form of spiritual (and political) union.

Toward the end of the war, Whitman met a former Confederate soldier, Peter Doyle, at the time a twenty-one-year-old streetcar conductor in Washington and later a railroad man, who came to be Walt's closest companion at mid-life. Doyle's family had emigrated from Ireland when he was eight years old and set-tled in Alexandria, Virginia. At the outbreak of the war, the seventeen-year-old Doyle enlisted and served for eighteen months as a Confederate artilleryman. At the battle of Antietam, he was aligned against forces that included Whitman's brother George. Doyle was apparently wounded in the battle and shortly thereafter discharged. He was arrested as he crossed Union lines going into Washington and put in prison but was soon released on his testimony that he was a British subject escaping the Confederacy and on promise that he would no longer aid the rebellion. He met Whitman on the streetcar one night early in 1865, and they were immediately drawn to one another. Members of Doyle's family remembered Peter as "a homosexual," and though Whitman struggled with his emotions about Doyle, worrying at times that his intensity was unrequited, he clearly loved the young man. Numerous accounts report their rides on the streetcar and their long walks and times together around Washington. The two men stayed in touch by writing letters when Whitman made his regular visits back to Brooklyn. It was Doyle who gave Whitman a first-hand account of Lincoln's assassination. After Whitman's stroke in 1873, Doyle took turns with Ellen O'Connor in nursing the poet. Though they always kept separate quarters, Whitman and Doyle were constantly together from their 1865 meeting until Whitman's bad health forced him to leave Washington for good. After that, they visited each other occasionally and exchanged letters. Whitman's letters to Doyle, along with an interview of Doyle, were published under the title *Calamus* by Whitman's biographer and disciple, Richard Maurice Bucke.[14]

The period of reflection and decline (1873–1892)

Whitman was devastated in 1873 by the death of his mother and the paralytic stroke that destroyed his own health. He was forced to leave Washington and live with the family of his brother George in Camden, New Jersey. For some time, he remained lonely and out of sorts, away from friends like Doyle and the O'Connors.

He recovered only gradually and never again attained his full power, his poetic inspiration declining along with his physical strength. Eventually he bought a house of his own on Mickle Street in Camden, where he lived until his death. He continued to make friends with young men, becoming particularly close to Harry Stafford, whose home Whitman visited in the country, where he found much of the material for the nature sketches in *Specimen Days*. And he entertained a growing stream of literary visitors and admirers. The psychiatrist and mystic Richard Maurice Bucke, who came from Canada, was Whitman's host on a northern excursion and became the poet's first biographer. Beginning in 1888, the same year that Thomas Eakins completed his celebrated portrait of Whitman, the young Horace Traubel, a journalist and political activist, became the poet's Boswell, sitting daily with the old man and recording their conversations in great detail, later collected as the multi-volume set *With Walt Whitman in Camden*. Visitors from abroad included Edward Carpenter and Oscar Wilde. Whitman corresponded with the likes of Alfred, Lord Tennyson, and received letters and articles about his work from other European writers.

One admirer's letter, addressed only "To Walt Whitman, America," found its way into his hands, much to the poet's delight.[15]

He continued to bring out new editions of *Leaves of Grass* – in 1867, 1871–2, 1881–2, and the "Deathbed Edition" in 1891–2. As a prose writer, he continued to advance his understanding of America's past and future and his philosophy of personality and art. Two reflective essays he published not long after the war, "Democracy" and "Personalism," were expanded into the 1871 volume *Democratic Vistas*. He merged *Memoranda During the War* with extensive reflections on nature, literature, philosophy, and travel to produce the memoir *Specimen Days*, published in 1882.

Whitman was in the company of his admirers when he died on 26 March 1892 at home in Camden.

Chapter 2

Historical and cultural contexts

In one of his last reflections on *Leaves of Grass*, the essay "A Backward Glance o'er Travel'd Roads," Whitman describes his original ambition: "to articulate and faithfully express in literary or poetic form, and uncompromisingly, my own physical, emotional, moral, intellectual, and aesthetic Personality in the midst of, and tallying, the momentous spirit and facts of . . . current America" (658). Whitman understood himself to embody in his poems and in his person the turmoil of a new nation struggling to define itself. This historical and poetic identity persisted, though not without its own turmoil and revisions, through the processes that came to define nineteenth-century US history – urbanization, industrialization, westward expansion, and war. It endured and was shaped by conflicts over race, class, gender, and culture.

In light of Whitman's identification with America, the history out of which *Leaves of Grass* grew is best understood not as mere "background" for the poems, but as a context in which the text is deeply rooted. Better yet, history and culture were "influences" in the literal sense of something that "flows in" to the work, or (to use two of Whitman's favorite terms) "rivulets" that "infused" the poetry. Whitman was not only a witness to the movements and events of his day but also a key participant: a country schoolteacher, a skilled worker, a city journalist, a companion to wounded soldiers in the Washington war hospitals, and a poet who formed a bardic conception of his role, giving voice to the currents and tides of historical change.

Accordingly, this chapter does not strictly separate the life and works from the historical context. It rather picks up threads from the biography (Chapter 1) and anticipates the discussion of Whitman's poetry and prose (Chapters 3, 4, and 5) with an overture of key historical themes: democracy, the body, the land, and the culture.

Democracy

Whitman appears at the mid-nineteenth century as an impassioned advocate for the common people and a strong critic of elitism in politics as well as in art and culture. His position was molded by the political values of the French and American Revolutions – above all, liberty, fraternity, and equality – which he inherited from his father's and grandfathers' generations. He came of age during the advent of Jacksonian democracy, a political program that increasingly involved greater segments of the working classes. His intellectual heritage also included literary Romanticism and liberal Protestantism, which contributed a deep strain of individualism – a belief in the basic integrity, if not the sanctity, of every person. Whitman's individualism, or personalism (as he sometimes called it), formed a dialectical relation with his faith in the American people en masse, so that poems like "Song of Myself" strive to reconcile individuality with the cause of union and community.

In his political life, the ideology of individualism reinforced a streak of stubborn self-reliance in his character that kept Whitman from ever becoming a successful Party man. A Democrat in his youth, he became disenchanted in the 1840s when the Party divided, largely (but not completely) along regional lines. Southern Democrats demanded the continuance of the slave economy and advocated a strong "state's rights" position, resisting the growing tendency of the federal government to encroach on the laws and undermine the self-rule of individual states. Northern Democrats generally shared the state's-rights principles of the southerners, but they often questioned the value of slavery. Their greatest worry was not so much that slavery was wrong in principle – the position of the more radical abolitionists – but that the integrity and the competitive power of northern labor was threatened by the existence of the slave economy. The conflict came to a head at mid-century as settlement expanded in the west and Congress had to decide whether each new state would be "slave" or "free."

Whitman believed that the future of America lay westward, so he balked at the idea of extending slavery to new states. His decision to leave the Democrats and join the Free-Soil Party was consistent with his commitment to working-class politics in the north. His experience as an artisan (a printer and carpenter) and his friendships with firemen and omnibus drivers – low-paid, hard-working city men whose names, addresses, and descriptions he kept in a notebook that survives from the 1850s – deepened his attachment to the laboring classes. Though he was himself part of a growing lower-middle class of literate urban and suburban professionals that included teachers, journalists, shopkeepers, and small-business owners, he remained committed to the political model of "artisanal republicanism," in which mechanics, skilled laborers, and free-holding small farmers were the ideal citizens. His ideal community involved the face-to-face interchanges typical of villages, small towns, and neighborhoods. Excited by the seeming opportunities for working people in the diverse and aggressive economy of the city, Whitman may have overlooked the dominant centralizing forces of big business and big government that accompanied urbanization. These forces would ultimately undo the independence of the working classes, leaving them vulnerable to the fluctuations of an international economy. Whitman's image of happy villagers lending a hand to build a new America seems sadly naïve in retrospect.[1]

Though he certainly objected to slavery, then, Whitman was never an abolitionist – much like Lincoln himself, who was known only after his death as the great emancipator. Even so, the slavery issue seems to have prompted specifically poetical impulses in Whitman's psyche. He heard Emerson speak on the topic in the late 1840s, mingling abolitionist politics with ideas on self-reliance that the young Whitman would certainly have found stimulating.[2] He addressed the slave question himself in his first efforts at political oratory and in many editorials. Also about this time, Whitman began to experiment in his notebooks with a new kind of poetic utterance, something like prose poetry, and to use the first-person persona "I" to test political positions different from the extreme voices of both abolitionists and defenders of slavery. "I am the poet of slaves and of the masters of slaves," he wrote, "And I will stand between the masters and the slaves, / Entering into both so that both shall understand me alike."[3]

By the late 1850s, the struggle over slavery and state's rights had devolved into actual bloodshed. In 1856, the abolitionist senator Charles Sumner of Massachusetts was beaten nearly to death on the Senate floor by an enraged opponent from South Carolina. In "Bleeding Kansas," John Brown led a group of militant Free-Soilers on a murderous rampage in retaliation for an attack on the town of Lawrence led by "Border Ruffians" from the slave state of Missouri. Disgusted with party politics and dismayed by the condition of the nation, Whitman wrote an angry pamphlet entitled "The Eighteenth Presidency!" to express his dissatisfaction with the administrations of Zachary Taylor and Franklin Pierce. Addressed to "Each Young Man in the Nation, North, South, East and West," the essay called for a new kind of President, a man from the working classes, someone not controlled by the parties. "The Eighteenth Presidency!" is memorable mainly for its inflammatory rhetoric and for its diehard belief that a hero will arise from the masses to lead America out of its dismal political condition. Discovered in proof sheets and never published in

Whitman's lifetime, the essay brings to the surface the political emotions that burn beneath the seeming equanimity and optimism of the early editions of *Leaves of Grass.*

Whitman's political fervor seems to have cooled somewhat in the late 1850s as he turned from political journalism to poetry as his chosen profession. With the outbreak of the Civil War in 1861, he all but retired from partisan politics. After the war, during the period known as Reconstruction, with corruption rampant and much of the country reeling from the cost of the war, there was precious little to celebrate. Whitman's postwar writings on democracy, such as *Democratic Vistas* (1871), are concerned more with the literary and spiritual implications of his political outlook. His love of common people and his belief that the future of democracy rested in their hands remained largely consistent throughout his life. But in his recorded conversations with young socialists like Horace Traubel, who were drawn to the barely submerged political fire of the early *Leaves of Grass,* the old poet seemed ambivalent about large-scale programs for social change and about radicalism in general. In final analysis, Whitman's most enduring contribution to American political thought and art may well be his personalization of political life in his poetry of the body.

The body

In *Leaves of Grass,* the body politic has its foundation in the politicized body. Anticipating the personalized politics of race and gender that inform much of public life in current times, Whitman portrayed the human body as a beautiful but embattled terrain.

The roots of his body politics appear most clearly in the 1855 version of "I Sing the Body Electric." In parallel sections of the poem, Whitman considers the plight of "A slave at auction" (123) and "A woman at auction" (124). The idea that a person's body can be bought, its essential strength and beauty commodi-fied, is a horror that Whitman insists his audience face directly, notwithstanding the good manners and conspiracy of silence that would prohibit the mention of the body and its parts in polite company, in "parlors and lecture-rooms" (123). This silencing and denial of the human body's regenerative power and undeniable attraction abet commodification, as does any form of morality or religion that would claim to save the soul while allowing the diminution of the body. Never denying the existence of the soul, Whitman confronts this pious hypocrisy by insisting on the sanctity of the body. "If life and the soul are sacred," he insists, "the human body is sacred" (124). And the bodies of slaves, prostitutes, and "dullfaced immigrants" are equally sacred (122).

Though his style may have shocked readers in his own time, the references to the twin evils of slavery and prostitution would have been a familiar pairing for Whitman's most immediate audience. Combined with the temperance movement – to which Whitman dedicated his early novel *Franklin Evans* – and later the women's movement, the opposition to slavery and prostitution formed the main platforms of the "social purity" movement in mid-nineteenth-century America. Social purity drew its energy from concerns over the moral and physical health of the nation as urbanization and geographical mobility seemed to weaken the local influences of family, community, and the church. Moving like other young men from country to city and back again, Whitman was a prime member of the audience to which the purity literature was directed – a young man on his own, tempted daily by alcohol, sex, and violent stimulations of various kinds.

Early on, he was attracted by the social purity movement. Working as a journalist in the big city, he became concerned with the problem of public health, writing editorials on the Brooklyn water supply and interviewing or attending lectures by well-known doctors and health advocates. He heard the warnings about the wrong diet (spicy foods and stimulants), the wrong associations (the mingling of the races and classes), and the wrong practices (everything from wearing tightly fitting clothes to masturbating). He wrote reviews of works by sexologists, medical writers, and moralists. He visited the phrenologists, who believed that moral character was revealed in the physical traits of the face and head. He had the bumps of his own cranium charted by the famous Lorenzo Fowler, whose phrenological firm of Fowler and Wells was eventually involved in publishing the 1856 *Leaves of Grass*. He followed developments in the women's movement and came to appreciate a new model of womanhood, which he called "a true woman of the new aggressive type," a type foreshadowed by his own hardworking mother and embodied in the women reformers he came to know – Abby Hills Price, Ernestine L. Rose, Paulina Wright Davis, Mary Chilton, and Eliza Farnham.[4]

The influences of the reformers played directly into Whitman's self-proclaimed status as the "poet of the body" in 1855. He took up not only the themes of the social purists but even their odd terminology and concepts. From phrenology he borrowed – and transformed – words like "amativeness" to describe the sexual love that passed between men and women and "adhesiveness" for the loving comradeship between men. From eclectic medical writers like Edward H. Dixon, he took the strange notion of sexual electricity, the idea that an actual electric charge passes between men and women during courtship and intercourse, and thus arrived at his concept of "the body electric."[5]

Although his poems had clear antecedents in the popular culture of his day, Whitman often seems to have written himself into a position more transgressive and radical than he himself might have admitted in conversation or in an editorial column. He was more of an abolitionist, more tolerant of ethnic differences and immigration, and more of a sexual rebel in *Leaves of Grass* than he ever permitted himself to be in his journalism and letters.

He seems also to have been more daring in his poetic expression of what twenty-first-century readers usually understand as an intense and undeniable homoeroticism. When confronted with questions about his intentions in the "Calamus" poems and his general portrayal of male–male love, he was either evasive or adamant in his denial of anything like homosexual intent. Yet by the end of the nineteenth century, references to Whitman and the use of his term "comrade" became almost a code for identification among the early advocates of gay consciousness and liberation. In the poet's own youth, it was perhaps easier to slip beneath the homophobic radar. Men commonly slept together and were more demonstrative in their public affection for one another than good manners permitted them to be with women. Whitman may have stretched the bounds of the "friendship tradition" in literature, but few contemporary reviewers called attention to any transgression, perhaps out of fear of even mentioning the possibility of sex between men. There was hardly a language for doing so. The word "homosexual" was not coined until the 1890s, and even the criminal term "sodomy" was known in the legal literature – usually in Latin – as "a crime not fit to be named among Christians," "the very mention of which is a disgrace to human nature."[6] The Latin version of this phrase appeared once in an early review of the 1855 *Leaves* by Rufus Griswold: "The records of crime show that many monsters have gone on in impunity, because the exposure of their vileness was attended with too great delicacy. *Peccatum illud horrible, inter Christianos non nominandum.*"[7]

Griswold's remarks suggest that while careful (and perhaps streetwise) readers could discern a hint of homosexuality in Whitman's poems, many may have been afraid or "too delicate" to broach the topic. The harshest criticism was reserved for his treatment of heterosexual desire in poems like "A Woman Waits for Me," which violated public mores by suggesting that female libido could be a match for male desire. His very mention of prostitution in the relatively tame "To a Common Prostitute" also drew fire. Ironically, several contemporary women readers, such as the Englishwoman Anne Gilchrist, found his view honest and invigorating even as the predominantly male reviewers chastised him.

In the years after the Civil War, with the loss of his own physical vigor, Whitman all but gave up writing the poetry of the body. But in such prose works as "A Memorandum at a Venture," he continued to defend his sexually forthright poems and insisted on the necessity of treating the body with candor and respect. Near the end of his life, he told Horace Traubel that "the eager physical hunger, the wish of that which we will not allow to be freely spoken of is still the basis of all that makes life worthwhile . . . Sex: Sex: Sex." Using an organic metaphor that hints at the place of sex in the whole scheme of his *Leaves*, he called sex "the root of roots: the life below the life."[8]

The land

In his memoir *Specimen Days*, Whitman reveals the importance of the land in his life and work. He says that "the combination of [his] Long Island birth-spot, sea-shores, childhood's scenes, absorptions, with teeming Brooklyn and New York" was one of the "formative stamps" upon his character (705–6). Far more than a setting for his poems, the natural and built environments of the North American seaboard amounted to an ecological niche for the poet and his *Leaves*.

Whitman's native region encompassed both rural and urban elements. What would become the great northeastern cities experienced huge influxes of population in Whitman's day as people regularly came from abroad or left the farm to seek new opportunities for wealth in the rapidly expanding economy of the cities. Whitman's family joined the migration – or rather the back-and-forth flow – from country to town. He ultimately settled in the city – first New York, then Washington, and finally Camden in the Philadelphia area. In writing of his life in these vibrant places, he earned the title of "America's first urban poet."[9] But he would return to the seashore of his Long Island home as a pilgrim returns to sacred ground, for self-renewal and reflection. The rural coastline and the city proved to be key sources of inspiration in many of his most memorable poems, such as "Out of the Cradle Endlessly Rocking" and "Crossing Brooklyn Ferry."

Though he shared with such contemporaries as Emerson, Bryant, Longfellow, and Whittier a predilection for nature poetry, Whitman is distinguished from his contemporaries by his celebration of the city. As an urban writer, he anticipates such modernist poets as T. S. Eliot, Marianne Moore, and Allen Ginsberg. Moreover, even in his treatment of nature, he varies from his Romantic predecessors. While the trend among the poets of his day was largely pastoral – a view of nature as the place of spirit, a site that offered relief from the stress and intensity of the materialist city, a more innocent and largely lost environment – *Leaves of Grass* treats the natural world as the body of the earth, an eroticized material entity with a character that alternately entices and resists the poet's curious questions and probings. The human body, with its spontaneously responsive and richly sensual impulses, is treated as continuous with nature. Whitman makes love to the land, pleads to the ocean as a child to its mother, looks curiously into the eyes of animals, and discovers in himself the same energies and materials that bring the earth to life. As much as his relation to the earth is material, it is also mystical. It identifies the self with this larger, more powerful, and only partially knowable entity. In his later work, especially *Specimen Days* but even in *Leaves of Grass*, Whitman would occasionally revert to a conventionally Romantic view of nature as an alternative to the modern life of the city. In this view, he anticipates the "back to nature" movement that came later in American culture. His more original outlook, however, involves an understanding of nature as integral and inescapable, as much a part of city life and the experience of the body as it is something separate, a nonhuman environment (literally "that which surrounds").

Whitman's alternation between an alienated view of the land (humanity distinct from nature) and the more integrated view (humanity continuous with nature) anticipated the dilemmas of environmentalism in the twentieth century. In the nineteenth century, the issues were already forming. Whitman's early journalism expresses his concern about the healthiness of the city environment – he worries over the impurity and unreliability of the water supply and the rapid spreading of disease, for example. In "Song of the Redwood-Tree," he struggled with problems known later as the loss of species and the conflict between labor and environmental protection. In "Passage to India" and *Democratic Vistas*, he praised technological achievement and material progress, but lamented that spirituality and culture lagged behind in development. Even as he celebrated diversity and equality, his enthusiasm for westward expansion in many of his works led him to embrace the language of imperialism and manifest destiny, the idea that people of European descent were destined by God and nature to bring their version of civilization to the rest of the world.[10]

In many ways, the difficulties that Whitman encountered with concepts of the land reflect the limits of his democratic politics. The land must belong to the people, but it cannot belong at once to Mexico and the US, nor to slaveowners and Free-Soilers – and what of the Native Americans displaced and destroyed by the policies of Andrew Jackson and other advocates of manifest destiny? What white easterners understood as wide-open spaces in the west were in fact the homes and hunting grounds of the indigenous tribes. These dilemmas are acknowledged but remain unresolved in Whitman's work. Under such headings as environmental justice and ecological racism, they continue to haunt political life in current times.

The culture

In his late-life reflections on what made him the poet he was, Whitman tended to emphasize his place of birth, the influence of his parents, and the Civil War. Of equal importance, however, were the cultural influences of the urban life in which he immersed himself beginning in early adulthood. To paraphrase Herman Melville's remark about whaling ships, the city streets were Whitman's Harvard and Yale.

It was in the city that Whitman faced new challenges and opportunities for his early-acquired habit of forming observations into language. His newspaper work required frequent encounters with the city's diverse population and daily participation in its highly varied events. The chance to argue about literature in reviews and personal encounters with other writers on the New York scene sped the development of his poetic and critical theories. He gained new perspectives and intellectual depth from the science, medicine, and technology he learned about in the books he reviewed, in public lectures, and in conversations with doctors and medical reformers. He supplemented his own direct experience of democratic politics with information and commentaries gathered from debates, pamphlets, party newspapers, and public oratory. He made the most of the city's many entertainments, attending the opera and theatre often and going to concerts of folk and classical music. He visited such attractions as Dr. Henry Abbot's Egyptian Museum on Broadway and the famous Crystal Palace Exhibition, which exposed the citizens of New York to an impressive display of painting, sculpture, and photography, as well as promoting American industry and technological development.

His early love of books intensified and expanded. From reading popular novels (by Walter Scott and George Sand, among others) and from writing fiction of his own, he cultivated a storyteller's imagination. From reading widely in English and American poetry (Shakespeare, Tennyson, and Bryant, for example) and writing conventional poems for the papers, he learned to express thoughts and emotions within the confines of poetic form. He looked deeply into Greek epic poetry and philosophy in translation and was fond of declaiming Homer from the seats he shared with the drivers of New York omnibuses. A passage from his notebooks shows his interest in Plato's conception of love and portrayal of male friendships. He made a close study of language, reading the latest theories and composing a set of fragmentary essays on US English, later edited by Horace Traubel and published posthumously as *An American Primer*.

One of the most powerful literary influences on *Leaves of Grass* was the King James Bible. Whitman always advocated a clear separation of church and state, and he looked with suspicion upon the influence of the paid clergy and organized religion. While never a practicing Christian, however, he still accepted many tenets of the faith – such as belief in God, the immortal soul, and life after death – and his best poetry attests to his deep familiarity with the Hebrew and Christian scriptures. The Psalms and prophetic books provided models for his free verse – the irregular line lengths, alternative rhythms, and highly varied patterns of repetition.[11] In creating his famous persona – the "Myself" of his "songs" – Whitman also drew upon the character of the Old Testament prophets and the person of Jesus. In "To a Common Prostitute," for example, the encounter of the speaker with the woman of the street recalls Jesus' defense of fallen women against the charges of the Jewish patriarchal establishment. And yet the poem's persona transforms the Gospel source nearly beyond recognition by claiming to speak more for nature than for God. "I am Walt Whitman," he says, "liberal and lusty as nature" (512).

This tendency to deify nature, as well as to transform his biblical sources, points to the writer of the period generally regarded as the strongest literary and philosophical influence on Whitman's work – Ralph Waldo Emerson. Emerson's imprint on Whitman's work is so clear that Whitman is sometimes included among the school of American Transcendentalists that looked to Emerson for inspiration and that included Henry David Thoreau among its leading lights. In essays like "Self-Reliance," Emerson gave Whitman the courage to pursue his own deepest insights. Whitman answered the call of Emerson's "American Scholar" to create a specifically American literary art that would represent in new forms the natural wonders and special character of life on the North American continent. Whitman's 1855 Preface owes much to Emerson's essay "The Poet," above all the concept of the poet as a kind of secular priest and prophet. The mystical experience of oneness with nature and all beings finds a similar expression in Emerson's *Nature* and Whitman's "Song of Myself," Section 5. And both authors insist that everyday life contains miracles as astounding as any recorded in the New Testament. Many of the tenets of English Romanticism and German Idealism probably first made their way into Whitman's work by way of Emerson's influence, although by the time of his late-life prose, when Whitman was struggling to get out from under Emerson's shadow, he showed his direct familiarity with many of the European writers, notably Carlyle and Hegel.

Where Whitman most clearly departed from Emerson and his closest follow-ers was in his devotion to the working class and his forthright treatment of the body. The urbane and college-educated Transcendentalists of New England, despite their admiration for Whitman's energy, were surprised on their visits to him in New York at the way he dressed and the company he kept. They prob-ably attributed his candor about sex and his bluntness in communication to his lower-class origins. Half in distaste and half in admiration, Thoreau wrote to a friend that he found *Leaves of Grass* "exhilarating" but also suggested that Whitman seemed incapable of higher emotions. He "does not celebrate love at all. It is as if the beasts spoke."[12] In his turn, Whitman considered Thoreau a bit stiff and disdainful of common people.

The Transcendentalist influence on Whitman is strongest in the Preface of 1855 and in "Song of Myself." In later editions, Whitman cultivated his dis-tinctive voice and drew upon new sources, particularly the visual arts. He loved painting, especially the French genre painters like Millet who captured the images of everyday life among ordinary people. But it was photography that really caught his interest, probably because it brought the promise of technol-ogy to the aid of the artist's eye. Perhaps the most frequently photographed nineteenth-century US author, Whitman was fascinated with the idea of a medium of representation so closely connected with the material reality of its subject. No photograph could be taken from memory or imagination. It required a direct existential connection with the thing or person it depicted. Whitman's enthusiasm for photography and visual culture in general becomes clear in his development of realism and the imagistic mode of poetry in his later writing.[13]

Whitman's poetry, like all literature, flowed out of its influences and sources and developed in a community of writers, readers, and critics. But Whitman's claim to originality remains a strong one. *Leaves of Grass* is a culture-bearing book that thoroughly transforms the forces of nineteenth-century artistic expression and carries them forward into modernity. It remains a phenomenon to be reckoned with by students and practitioners of poetry down to the present.

Chapter 3

Poetry before the Civil War

American poetry underwent a profound shift with the publication of *Leaves of Grass*. It is only a slight exaggeration to say that, with this book, Walt Whitman changed the shape of poetry. He all but invented free verse in English, introducing breathlessly long lines and using repetition of words and sounds to create a web-like form to replace the conventional meters used by even the most experimental poets before him. He stretched the democratic poetics he inherited from Romanticism to new extremes, abandoning traditional diction while creating a style that mingled the language of everyday life with bold ventures into figural expression. He likewise embraced subject matter normally considered outside the scope of poetry, including "low" topics associated with the experience of the human body, sexuality, and the life of the streets. As a poetry of nature, *Leaves of Grass* served as a watershed for the main streams of Romantic and Transcendentalist writing and thought. But Whitman's book also embodied the struggles of a nation confronted with ethnic and class conflict, modernization, total war, urbanization, industrialization, and finally globalization.

This chapter deals with the poems composed for the first three editions of *Leaves of Grass* – 1855, 1856, and 1860. Whitman began the decade of the fifties with a burst of hopeful energy. Building on the spirit of the European Revolutions of 1848 and catching the fever of Jacksonian democracy and westward expansion, with its promise of nearly unlimited range for the development of the democratic way of life, the poet concocted an expansive theory of selfhood that informed and inspired the great cosmic/dramatic poems of 1855 and 1856, including "Song of Myself," "The Sleepers," and "Crossing Brooklyn Ferry."

So dominant is the optimistic mood of these poems in *Leaves of Grass* that William James, drawing upon Richard Maurice Bucke's account of Whitman's mystical illumination, would see the poet as the main exemplar of a variety of religious experience that James called "healthymindedness" – "an inability to feel evil."[1] What James failed to recognize, or at least articulate, is that the hopeful side of Whitman's vision is balanced (and to some extent stimulated) by a strong sense of dread and anxiety, largely stemming from an ominous fear that political conflicts were on the verge of tearing the nation apart. In many ways, the poems of "healthymindedness" constitute a kind of wishful thinking and restless energy, rooted in an anxious desire to save the nation from self-destruction. As Chapters 1 and 2 showed, the turmoil of the times seemed to match the personal conflicts Whitman felt over his difficulties in finding an appreciative audience for his writings and over questions of his sexual identity. What began as a decade of positive, creative energy ended in depression arising from political disillusionment, masculine self-doubt, and the fear of failure, reflected in the elegiac tone of the poems published in 1860, such as "As I Ebb'd with the Ocean of Life," "Out of the Cradle Endlessly Rocking," and many of the "Calamus" poems. These works invoke a deep and troubling sense of loss or alienation alongside a weaker sense of reconciliation than we find in the cosmic/dramatic poems of 1855 and 1856. In the 1860 poems, the style remains expansive and the language bold and highly figured, but the poems also evince a greater use of symbols, a broad operatic sweep to the drama, ritual echoes from the poetic tradition, and a more solemn tone.

In offering readings of individual poems, this chapter does not pretend to be exhaustive, both for practical reasons (involving both space limitations and the length of many of the poems) and for theoretical ones (no single reading can exhaust the meaning of a poem). Moreover, the approach taken here is less concerned with what the poetry *means* or what it *is* and more concerned with what it *does*. This method draws on recent scholarship that connects Whitman's writing with the philosophy of American pragmatism, which had roots in Emersonian thought and emerged full-blown in the generation after Whitman, notably in the work of Charles Sanders Peirce, William James, and John Dewey. Whitman anticipates some key premises of philosophical pragmatism – that knowledge and even being are best understood as the outcome of action or practice, that experience rather than essence shapes the human condition in everything from education to politics, that variety and diversity should be embraced rather than suppressed or discouraged, and that human understanding at all times is tentative and fallible. The pragmatic approach dovetails nicely with a widely acknowledged view of Whitman's language that derives from speech-act theory. According to this view, his poems favor the kind of "performative" language seen in vows and oaths. The poems "do things with words" and render a world in action rather than making definitive statements about a static world. Whitman's language and world view are thus relational, dynamic, and dramatic rather than doctrinal and propositional. By focusing on certain movements within each poem, the readings offered here are intended to be open-ended and incomplete. They open the way to other readings and hint at further poetic accomplishments.

1855: "Song of Myself"

The poem ultimately known as "Song of Myself" appears only under the repeated title of "Leaves of Grass" in 1855. It dominates the first edition and is considered by many critics to be Whitman's masterpiece. It is the certainly the longest poem he ever wrote and remains in all editions the most comprehensive. In style and subject matter, it anticipates almost every turn in Whitman's mature poetic development but also exhibits a number of features that make it unique in the Whitman corpus. Its centrality to *Leaves of Grass* involves, among other accomplishments, its experimentation in form and style, its development of a fluid persona embodying Whitman's theories of the self within a democratic union, its celebration of a mystical experience that merges spirituality with the experience of sexuality and the body, its use of catalogues of images and expanded vignettes to explore the range of experience within modern life, and its exploration of the limits of human knowledge and language. The reading that follows considers each of these movements and the thematic and formal connections among them.

The poem conducts a radical experiment in poetic form

In "Song of Myself," Whitman experiments with his mode of expression at all levels – word, phrase (or line), section (or stanza), and whole text. What would later become relatively fixed genres, poetic modes, or rhetorical strategies for him – the cosmic/prophetic mode of "Crossing Brooklyn Ferry," the elegiac/introspective mode of "Out of the Cradle Endlessly Rocking" and "When Lilacs Last in the Dooryard Bloom'd," and the imagistic mode of "Cavalry Crossing a Ford" and "The Dalliance of the Eagles" – appear to vie for dominance within the poetic laboratory of "Song of Myself." The reader seems to catch the various modes of expression in the act of formation, highly dynamic and volatile.

At the level of the word and phrase, Whitman foregoes the standard language of elevated poetic diction (the "thees" and "thous" and other archaisms still used in British Victorian poetry, for example) and favors instead the ordinary language of American conversation with a strong mix of foreign terms, colloquialisms, place names, technical terms, slang, and new words he creates himself with innovative uses of prefixes and endings. A sample of the oddities would include *loafe, kelson, savans, embrouchures, vivas, veneralee, foofoos, kosmos, duds,* and *accoucheur.*[2] He often mingles formal and informal diction, as in Section 6 of "Song of Myself" when he calls the grass "a uniform hieroglyphic" that grows the same "among black folks as among white, / Kanuck, Tuckahoe, Congressman, Cuff," using colloquial expressions for people from different regions and ethnic types (193). His figurative language stretches the bounds of common sense and poetic practice – confusing anatomical references to the heart and genitals, for example, and muddying distinctions between body and soul, male and female, animal and mineral.

At the level of the phrase, line, and stanza, Whitman's experiment goes yet further. Rather than the arbitrary limits that traditional versification places upon syllable number, stress pattern, or number of lines, the phrase itself seems to determine the length of lines in Whitman's verse while shifts in topic, perspective, or voice drive the stanza breaks, as in prose paragraphs. The lines tend to be long, and line and stanza length are highly irregular and variable. The clearest model for this experiment is the King James Bible, but Whitman's free verse also mimics the cadences and rhythms of oratorical prose. Indeed one of the boundaries Whitman challenges in *Leaves of Grass* is that between prose and poetry. The prose of the 1855 Preface was sufficiently poetic to be, in the 1856 edition, incorporated into the poem later titled "By Blue Ontario's Shore." The highly varied lines and phrases in "Song of Myself" are held together by repetitive devices such as assonance and alliteration, syntactic parallelism, and repetition of key words and phrases, especially at the beginning of lines (using the rhetorical device of anaphora).

In the larger scheme of the whole poem, Whitman blends the genres of epic and lyric poetry. Echoing the opening of Virgil's *Aeneid* – "Of arms and the man I sing" – Whitman's famous first line, "I CELEBRATE myself, and sing myself" (188), transforms the epic genre as surely as it alludes to it, fusing the functions of hero and bardic poet in the self-reflexive "I," and introducing the element of personal involvement usually associated with lyric poetry. The lyric side of the poem is further manifested in the variable moods of the poem's persona or speaker. He performs a shamanic or prophetic role in such lines as "I know that the hand of God is the promise of my own" (192) and "I pass death with the dying and birth with the new-wash'd babe, and am not contain'd between my hat and boots" (194). He bears witness as a casual bystander, "amused, complacent, compassionating, idle, unitary . . . curious what will come next . . . Both in and out of the game" (191), and makes reports as the journalist or public servant might: "The suicide sprawls on the bloody floor of the bedroom, / I witness the corpse with its dabbled hair, I note where the pistol has fallen" (195). He takes the part of the hero, boasting like Beowulf, but winking at his own hyperbole in such lines as "Whimpering and truckling fold with powders for invalids, conformity goes to the fourth-remov'd, / I wear my hat as I please indoors or out" (206) and "Divine am I inside and out, and I make holy whatever I touch or am touch'd from, / The scent of these arm-pits aroma finer than prayer" (211). He superimposes himself onto the characters of American history, past and present: "Alone far in the wilds and mountains I hunt" (196); "I am the hounded slave, I wince at the bite of the dogs" (225). At various points, the bardic voice returns to narrate the history of the nation, as in the vignettes of the Goliad Massacre in the war for Texas's independence from Mexico (226–7) and the "old-time sea-fight" of John Paul Jones in the War of 1812 (227–8).

The poem embodies the ideals of personality within the context of political democracy

Thus expanding the role of the bard as the bearer of culture, Whitman represents the people of America in at least three senses. As a writer represents a topic, he reproduces the nation in art. As an elected official represents a constituency in a republic, he speaks for the nation in the voice of an individual citizen. And as a hero represents the aspirations of the populace as a whole, he models the fullest experience of selfhood. This diverse development of the poem's main voice, "Myself," is as significant to the poem's psychology and politics as it is to Whitman's experiment in poetic form. It radically extends the sympathetic imagination associated with eighteenth-century poetics and the English Romantic poets, the tendency of which is to identify with others to the point of empathetic self-transformation. This fluidity of personality is dramatized, for example, in the interplay of "I" and "you" throughout the poem. The poet seems to overwhelm the reader in the second line – "And what I assume you shall assume" – but immediately qualifies the assertion by allowing that "every atom belonging to me as good belongs to you" (188). In this way, the poet–reader interchange becomes the first instance of a key theme in the poem – what Whitman calls the "knit of identity" (190) or "the merge." "Who need be afraid of the merge?" he asks in an 1855 line later removed from the text (33).

Throughout the poem, boundaries between self and others – boundaries of time, place, language, identity, and social distinction – dissolve as the poet unfolds visions of personal, political, and metaphysical union. The merge is of course figurative but also surprisingly literal. Just as "every atom of my blood" is "form'd from this soil," so is "your" blood formed; and just as the speaker was "born here of parents born here from parents the same," so has the reader been born of a particular lineage in some native place (188). The shared grounding of birth in the homeland, and more generally in the earth, is extended to include the sharing of atoms in the air in Section 2, which begins with the poet growing intoxicated on the "distillation" of rooms "full of perfumes" and ends with the poet's injunction that the reader should "filter" all things from the self, to distill it down to its basic substance (188–90). This odd interchange between the literal and the figurative is most perfectly realized in Section 6 in which the grass is said to "transpire" (literally breathe forth) from the buried bodies of dead men and women: "the beautiful uncut hair of graves" (193). The corpses literally feed into the grass and are transformed not only metaphorically but biologically, leading the poet to conclude, "The smallest sprout shows there is really no death" (194). The human self and nonhuman nature ultimately converge as one being.

The theme of the merge evolves as a wavelike, cyclical movement of blending and separation, identification and distinction. The movement is dramatized in the image from Section 3 of the "hugging and loving bed-fellow" who "sleeps at my side through the night, and withdraws at the peep of the day with stealthy tread" (191). The departing lover leaves "baskets cover'd with white towels swelling the house with their plenty" (191). This characteristic image suggests not only a gift of rising bread dough left for the lover now sleeping alone, but also the "swelling" of a figurative pregnancy, recalling the lines from Section 2: "Urge and urge and urge / Always the procreant urge of the world" (190). "Pro-creation" is practically a synonym for all sexual activity, whether reproductive or not, in the nineteenth century, an age in which birth control was virtually unknown and certainly ineffective. The sexual impulse is the force that drives the merge, which depends upon an acceptance of the body's goodness and health: "Welcome is every organ and attribute of me, and of any man hearty and clean, / Not an inch nor a particle of an inch is vile, and none shall be less familiar than the rest" (190–1).

The political uses of the sympathetic merge become clear by Section 19, in which the democratic spirit is represented in "the grass that grows wherever the land is and the water is . . . the common air that bathes the globe" (204). Section 20 states explicitly the theme implicit in the poem's opening lines: "In all people I see myself, none more and not one a barley-corn less" (206). In Section 21, the poet's inclusiveness extends to gender ("I am the poet of the woman the same as the man") and to metaphysics as well as material life ("I am the poet of the Body and I am the poet of the Soul, / The pleasures of heaven are with me and the pains of hell are with me"), and to the whole of the earth, personified as the poet's welcome lover: "Far-swooping elbow'd earth – rich apple-blossom'd earth! / Smile, for your lover comes" (207–8).

Picking up a theme from the 1855 Preface, the poet says in Section 21, "I chant the chant of dilation or pride" (207), a claim he balances in Section 22: "I am he attesting sympathy" (209). For Whitman and his contemporaries, "pride" would have meant, among other things, the tendency to impose the self onto the world (to "dilate" and "absorb") while "sympathy" would have suggested the contrary tendency to suppress the self and allow external forces (nature and ideas as well as other people) to shape one's identity. "I find one side a balance and the antipodal side a balance," says the poet, "Soft doctrine as steady help as stable doctrine" (209).

The expansive, alternately prideful and sympathetic movements of individualism and democracy are fully realized in the celebration that forms Section 24, the heart of the poem. The section begins with the poet's famous naming of himself, "Walt Whitman, a kosmos, of Manhattan the son" (210). He is at once an outcropping of the universal world soul, a "kosmos", and a particular, local phenomenon, "of Manhattan the son" – a body no less than a soul, animal as much as human: "Turbulent, fleshy, sensual, eating, drinking, and breeding" (210). Above all, he is democratic and egalitarian, "no stander above men and women or apart from them" (210). In the 1855 version of this line, he displays a special identity with the working class and the lower levels of society – "Walt Whitman, an American, one of the roughs, a kosmos" (50). Although he abandons his explicit affiliation with "the roughs" by the final version of the poem, perhaps in the search for an ever wider application of democratic sympathy, he continues to pursue an unrelenting egalitarianism, rooting political identity in the "primeval" body and the theory of democracy: "I speak the pass-word primeval, I give the sign of democracy, / By God! I will accept nothing which all cannot have their counterpart of on the same terms" (211).

The poem spiritualizes the body and materializes the soul in an effort to reinvigorate the religious experience

Section 24 also enfolds the shamanic role and enacts the upside-down mysticism that brings the poet closer to the earth rather than transporting him to some heaven. In his claim that "Whoever degrades another degrades me" (210), he echoes the attitudes of Jesus and Buddha – Jesus in his insistence that whatever is done to the least of his brothers is done also to him, and Buddha in his incarnation as the Bodhisattva who refuses to attain enlightenment until others can have the same. The poet channels the voices of others through his own voice, like a man possessed – the "many long dumb voices" of "interminable generations of prisoners and slaves," of "thieves and dwarfs," and "of the rights of them the others are down upon". He includes "the deform'd, trivial, flat, foolish, despised," right down to the lowest, most accursed conditions of nature: "Fog in the air, beetles rolling balls of dung" (211). These reflections bring him to the very root of human shame and separation from nature – the disgust for the body and the fear of death, which Whitman dispatches in a single line, using a term for sex normally reserved for animals: "Copulation is no more rank to me than death is" (211). Among the "forbidden voices" channeled through him are "voices of sexes and lusts," which if "indecent" are "by me clarified and transfigur'd" (211). For him, "Seeing, hearing, feeling, are miracles, and each part and tag of me is a miracle" (211). "Divine am I inside and out," he says, building steam toward a litany of admiration for the body's beauty: "If I worship one thing more than another it shall be the spread of my own body, or any part of it" (211). His egalitarianism extends to the despised or neglected parts of the human body as much to every constituent of the body politic. He portrays the body as both a metaphorical landscape ("shaded ledges") and the means for cultivating the land (the phallus appearing as a "masculine colter," that is, the blade of a plough) (211–12). The metaphors proliferate to the point where it becomes difficult to distinguish which part is figurative and which part literal, suggesting a mutuality of human and natural being. Is the "timorous pond-snipe" and "nest of guarded duplicate eggs" (212) a figure for the poet's own genitals or an actual observation of a swamp bird on its nest that arouses through its shape and movement the phallic impression? Substitutions and metonymies abound. Breezes that might ordinarily be described as tickling the nude body instead take on a body of their own: "Winds whose soft-tickling genitals rub against me" (212). The litany reaches a climax (in every sense of the word) with a vision of a fully phallicized cosmos: "Something I cannot see puts upward libidinous prongs, / Seas of bright juice suffuse heaven" (212).

While necessary, however, the body is not sufficient. The soul must also be "clear and sweet": "Lack one lacks both, and the unseen is proved by the seen" (190). In this light, the image of the swelling baskets in Section 3 hints at the Christian story of Jesus' feeding the five thousand from a few baskets of fish and bread. Everyday life, Whitman suggests, is not only good and pleasurable; it is full of miracles. As he proclaims in Section 31, with typical hyperbolic humor, "a mouse is miracle enough to stagger sextillions of infidels" (217). As he says in the 1855 Preface, "folks expect of the poet to indicate more than the beauty and dignity which always attach to dumb real objects. . . . they expect him to indicate the path between reality and their souls" (10; punctuation as in original).

The influence of Christian texts and concepts, such as the dualism of body and soul, immortality, and miracles, is clear in these lines. Equally clear, however, is that Whitman's treatment of body and soul differs strongly from mainstream Christianity. He rejects, for example, the notion of heaven and hell as states of future reward and punishment. There "will never be any more perfection than there is now," he says, "Nor any more heaven or hell than there is now" (190). Neither could he be satisfied with the linear and teleological assumptions of the Judeo-Christian tradition, as he indicates in his rejection of "the talk of the beginning and the end." In "Song of Myself," Whitman focuses on the present rather than the past or future, which he sees as contained in the mystical now: "There was never any more inception than there is now, / . . . And will never be any more perfection than there is now" (190).

The concept is powerfully dramatized in the famous Section 5, which appears to be an account of mystical illumination that adds elements of the dream vision to the expanding lyric-epic form. Beginning "I believe in you my soul," the passage appears to be a modern version of the medieval genre, the debate of body and soul (192). As the passage progresses, however, "I" and "you" accrue ambiguity, suggesting many possible pairs – the body and the soul, the poet and the reader, or the lyric poet and his real or imagined lover. Recalling the line from Section 1, "I loafe and invite my soul" (188), the speaker (body) invites the lover or fellow singer (soul) to "Loafe with me on the grass, loose the stop from your throat," to join in a primal union that eludes language – "Not words, not music or rhyme I want, not custom or lecture, not even the best, / Only the lull I like, the hum of your valvèd voice" (192). The repetition of the liquid l's and the humming m's suggests the ecstatic moaning of the lover as well as the voicing of the mystic "OM" chanted in yogic meditation. And instead of debate, we get seduction; the enlightenment merges into sexual experience, one experience informing and transforming the other. The mutual "loafing" and mingling of voices yield to the memory or fantasy of "how once we lay such a transparent summer morning": "How you settled your head athwart my hips and gently turn'd over upon me, / And parted the shirt from my bosom-bone, and plunged your tongue to my bare-stript heart" (192). These heated lines defy particularization. The position of the lovers' bodies suggests oral sex, particularly fellatio – "you . . . reach'd till you felt my beard, and reached till you held my feet" (192) – but the anatomy is anything but clear. The "plunging" of the tongue to the "bare-stript heart" mingles hints of kissing and cunnilingus with the mainstay of sentimental romance, the throbbing of the heart, the supposed center of emotional experience. Whitman figuratively strips the heart bare; that is, he associates it with the language of nearly pornographic sensuality, transforming the dominant sentimentalism of his age with material intensity.

The wild figures of these lines make the familiar strange and create a kaleidoscopic shifting of perspectives. The aim appears to be the representation of alternate states of perception, as in the mystical experience, and alternative versions of sexual experience. They take the poet "out of himself" much in the manner that Emerson describes in the famous "transparent eyeball" passage from *Nature*. Walking across a bare common, he says, "in snow puddles, at twilight, under a clouded sky, without having in my thoughts any occurrence of special good fortune, I have enjoyed a perfect exhilaration . . . I become a transparent eyeball; I am nothing; I see all; I am part or parcel of God." In the process of transformation, he says, "all mean egotism vanishes."[3] Whitman's transformation – which differs from Emerson's by engaging the whole body rather than limiting the experience to the sense of sight – involves perceiving the unity of the self with God ("the spirit of God is the brother of my own"), with other human beings ("all the men ever born are also my brothers, and the women my sisters and lovers"), and all creation. Indeed the elements of creation appear in images that mirror the elements of his own body – the pores of the skin reflected in "brown ants in the little wells beneath them," and the phallus mirrored in "the leaves stiff or drooping in the fields." Spreading out before him is "the peace and knowledge that pass all the argument of the earth," the knowledge that "a kelson of the creation is love" ("kelson" referring to a strengthening timber that runs along the keel of big ships) (192). The unity with God, all people, the body, and nature creates a metaphysical foundation for the democratic sentiments of the poem, thus launching the "myself" persona into the role of poet-prophet of democracy.

The calm that follows the intensity of the illumination – "the peace and knowledge that pass all the argument of the earth" – also suggests the restfulness, the "loafing" attitude of the body after sex. The mood extends into Section 6, in which the poet patiently reflects on the question of a child, "What is the grass"? (192). He runs through a number of possible answers, modeling an open-ended interpretive method that frees readers to "filter" each image for themselves and refusing to impose a definiteness of understanding. He allows the grass and other such things of nature to maintain something of their own integrity, the something that human consciousness can never fully "absorb" or master but can only "guess" at. His caution or tentativeness in this regard distinguishes him from Romantic predecessors like Emerson and Wordsworth, who more confidently read the book of Nature. For Whitman, the grass is alternately "the flag of my disposition, out of hopeful green stuff woven"; "the handkerchief of the Lord, / A scented gift and remembrancer designedly dropt" (to catch the attention of human lovers, "that we may see and remark, and say *Whose?*"); a child itself, "the produced babe of the vegetation"; an emblem of democracy, "a uniform hieroglyphic . . . Sprouting alike in broad zones and narrow zones, / Growing among black folks as among white"; and finally "the beautiful uncut hair of graves," the sign of immortality in the shared life of all natural beings (193). Section 7 reiterates the theme of immortality and its evidence in the beauty of all the things that life has to offer and of all people without exception, all "lips that have smiled, eyes that have shed tears" (194), all bodies – "Undrape! you are not guilty to me, nor stale nor discarded, / I see through the broadcloth and gingham whether or no" (195).

The poem uses catalogues of images and vignettes to suggest the open-ended and endlessly varied range of experience within modern life

The seeing poet unfolds a series of images in Sections 8–10, a celebration of sights and sounds of the teeming city, the baby sleeping in the cradle, the suicide victim sprawling dead on the floor, the blushing boy and girl in the meadow, the "blab of the pave, tires of carts, sluff of boot-soles, talk of the prome-naders" – "I mind them," he says, "or the show or resonance of them – I come and I depart" (195). This is the first of the famous "catalogues" in "Song of Myself," instances of the "enumerative style" that list impressions and images with and without commentary, often at great length. The catalogues have variously entranced, amused, irritated, bored, and puzzled readers since their first publication, inspiring admiration, condemnation, some imitation, and a great deal of parody. Whatever the response of readers, the technique is central to *Leaves of Grass* in every edition but is most prominent in the poems of the fifties.

Whitman follows Homer in using catalogues to lend an epic breadth and sweep to his vision. But his lists also have newer and deeper political and poetic implications. For the democratic poet, the attempt to all but exhaust a field of vision suggests that all people deserve attention and recognition. For the urban poet – the *flaneur* or aimless rambler absorbing the sights and energies of the city – cataloguing captures the experience of walking through the streets, taking account of faces old and new, getting the news, and relating oneself to the ever-changing display of people and scenes. For the transcendental poet of nature in the age of science, the earth deserves no less attention. Everything is potentially meaningful and connected at the deepest levels. The lists take the speaker out of himself and bring the richness of varied impressions into the self. He touches upon the items in each list lightly, the catalogue moving over the immediate impressions as a hand might caress the body of a loved one or a set of cherished objects. He is, as he says in Section 13, "the caresser of life . . . not a person or object missing, / Absorbing all to myself and for this song" (199). The flowing images likewise present to the mutually creative reader a world of material ready-made for poetic participation – and in this way, each compressed image within the catalogues anticipates the imagistic and impressionistic direction of his later poems.

As the poem cycles through the images, they undergo contraction and expansion as the poet seems to pass quickly or linger. An uneven but definite rhythm develops. In Section 10, for example, the movement slows and the images expand into five brief narratives. Short scenes of hunting, sailing, and digging clams are followed by slightly longer vignettes of the marriage of a trapper "in the open air in the far west" to a "red girl" and the hiding of a runaway slave by the speaker of the poem who takes the part of an engineer on the underground railroad (the network that supported the passage of escaped slaves moving from the south to the north) (196–7). The two scenes are related in involving contact between different races. Both involve a degree of tension. The differences in the dress and demeanor of the trapper and his Indian hosts and his grip upon the hand of his bride – as well as the power relations implicit in the conqueror taking a bride among the conquered – hint at some uneasiness in what might otherwise seem an idyllic portrait of democratic union on the frontier. The willingness of the northern householder to entertain the fugitive slave is likewise accompanied by the "revolving eyes" and "awkwardness" of the slave, not to mention the "fire-lock" leaning in the corner (197). Whether the speaker means to emphasize the threat of the gun in the eyes of the guest, or the possibility that violence might be needed to defend against the slave's pursuers, or merely the disuse of the gun as the black man sits next to the host at the dinner table remains ambiguous.

Expanding into an even fuller vignette, indeed becoming what amounts to a stand-alone poem, Section 11 picks up the theme of the contact narratives in musing on the most common social distinction of all – the difference between the genders. The vignette is narrated in the third person but from the perspective of a woman who "owns the fine house by the rise of the bank" and "hides handsome and richly drest aft the blinds of the window," watching as "Twenty-eight young men bathe by the shore," the number matching her "Twenty-eight years of womanly life and all so lonesome" (197). In taking the perspective of the woman, Whitman offers either a subversion or an outright transgression of the gender norms of his day. Subversively, he suggests that regardless of restrictions on "womanly life," fantasy runs rampant beneath the surface:

"Where are you off to, lady? for I see you, / You splash in the water there, yet stay stock still in your room" (197). And the fantasy is no mere sentimental idyll, but a full-blown and sexually charged vision, virtually masturbatory in its intensity: "They do not know who puffs and declines with pendant and bending arch, / They do not think whom they souse with spray" (198). A yet more transgressive reading would see the male poet's performing the woman's fantasy as an act of imaginative cross-dressing – the "womanly life" of the big house's owner meaning that "she" is kept from participation in the group swim by the requirements of class and a self-protective masculinity. A submerged homosexual desire is released by the fantasy of becoming the "twenty-ninth bather" who can move unrecognized among the carefree swimmers. "They do not ask . . . They do not know . . . They do not think." Perhaps better than any other, the episode embodies the sexual ambiguity and rebellious energy of the 1855 edition.

Sections 12–16 go back to the cataloguing of compressed images – the butcher-boy, the blacksmith, the negro driver, the wood-duck, the "sharp-hooved moose." The rambling speaker flows from human to animal, from city to countryside, and then out to the whole nation, extending his territory. Images expand slightly, then contract again to lists with each impression confined to a single long line. Occasionally, the speaker pauses to reflect. The "Ya-honk" of the wild goose, for example, sounds to him like an invitation: "The pert [or impertinent] may suppose it meaningless, but I listening close, / Find its purpose and place up there toward the wintry sky" (199). The lines that separate human from animal dissolve in the poet's sympathetic imagination.

The poem pushes the limits of human knowledge and language

Section 25 sounds the theme of vocal, creative power yearning to articulate and elaborate the "something" just beyond the limits of human knowledge, stretching the bounds of consciousness and perception: "My voice goes after what my eyes cannot reach, / With the twirl of my tongue I encompass worlds and volumes of worlds" (213). The great age of oratory and visionary prophesy finds expression in Whitman's notion that "Speech is the twin of my vision" (213). But finally, words are insufficient – "Writing and talk do not prove me" – and the experience of the mystical self remains ineffable though nonetheless real: "With the hush of my lips I wholly confound the skeptic" (214). In silence, he opts to "do nothing but listen" in Section 26 and is rewarded with a wealth of rich sounds, ranging from the sounds of the street to the singing of the grand opera, catalogued lovingly for the reader (214).

In Section 27, he shifts his focus to the sense of touch, which he finds particularly intense: "To touch my person to some one else's is about as much as I can stand" (215). The reflection leads in Section 28 to the vignette beginning "Is this then a touch? quivering me to a new identity" (215). The scene can be read either as a masturbatory fantasy – "I went myself first to the headland, my own hands carried me there" (216) – or an orgy of sexual initiation. The "prurient provokers" that appear "on all sides" could be a metaphor for the many sources of stimulation in modern life (particularly urban life, though the scene takes place in the countryside) or actual sexual partners "straining the udder of my heart for its withheld drip" (the heart again substituting for the genitals, as in Section 5). The setting in the outdoors on a headland (a meadow above a sea cliff) suggests the childhood home of the poet on the Long Island shore and may represent elements of his own adolescence, his entrance into sexual awareness. His defenses fall – "The sentries desert every other part of me" – and "given up by traitors," he submits to either his own fantasies of gang rape or the act itself (216). He is at once betrayed by his own sensitive touch and responsive body – "Treacherous tip of me reaching and crowding to help them" (215) – and beset by others, "the herd" that is "all uniting to stand on a headland and worry me" (216).

As in Section 5 and 24, the narrative climax of the episode – "You villain touch! what are you doing? my breath is tight in its throat, / Unclench your floodgates, you are too much for me" (216) – is the climax of the sexual act. Section 29 returns to the calm of relieved sexual tension and the poet's impression of an eroticized nature to match his own experience – "Landscapes projected masculine, full-sized and golden" (216). "A minute and a drop of me settle my brain," he explains provocatively in Section 30, connecting the mystical and the masturbatory, and then returns in Section 31 to the kind of transcendent vision already seen in Section 5 (217). Now a leaf of grass appears as "the journey-work of the stars" and the "running blackberry" vine beautiful enough to "adorn the parlors of heaven" (217). In what is usually read as an early reference to the theory of evolution, the poet claims that time and nature (mineral, vegetable, and animal) are perfected and embodied in his own being, reaching to attain its fullest realization: "I find I incorporate gneiss, coal, long-threaded moss, fruits, grains, esculent roots, / And am stucco'd with quadrapeds and birds all over" (217). Section 32 extends the vision with a celebration of the animals: "They do not sweat and whine about their condition, / They do not lie awake in the dark and weep for their sins" (218). In his transcendent calm, the poet sees that the animals "bring me tokens of myself" – "tokens" meaning mementos or rough representations, signs "of myself" (218). The "gigantic beauty of a stallion" whom he catches and rides brings back the images of sexual ecstasy and satisfaction in a brief vignette, with the clear suggestion this time of same-sex love, the stallion and his male rider the poet: "His nostrils dilate as my heels embrace him, / His well-built limbs tremble with pleasure as we race around and return." With the end of the ride comes release, suggesting a free and even promiscuous exchange: "I but use you a minute, then I resign you, stallion" (219).

To some extent, the structure of the entire poem follows the pattern of development surrounding the climactic Sections 5, 24, and 28. A period of rising tension leads to a "fit" of intense passion, then climax and calm, with the final stage producing a vision of cosmic unity and goodness. In other words, the cyclic structure of "Song of Myself" mimics the sexual experience of the human male, at least as Whitman conceived it. With each iteration of the pattern, the range of the vision increases. Following the ride on the stallion, the poet seems to float away from the earth in Section 33. He is "afoot with [his] vision." "My ties and ballasts leave me," he says, "my elbows rest in sea-gaps, / I skirt Sierras," and looking down, as if from a hot-air balloon, "my palm covers continents" (219). From this height, he offers a catalogue of images running from the farm to the frontier, occasionally dipping down and taking a role himself: "I am a free companion, I bivouac by invading watchfires, / I turn the bridegroom out of bed and stay with the bride myself" (224). He becomes the "hounded slave," the "mash'd fireman with breast-bone broken," an "old artillerist" (225–6). He floats as readily through time as through space, reporting on the Goliad massacre in Section 34 and the "old-time sea-fight" of John Paul Jones in Sections 35–7.

Enacting another pattern of the poem's structure – the interchange of openness to influence ("sympathy") and self-sufficiency ("pride") – he returns by Section 39 to ask of his own central role, "The friendly and flowing savage, who is he?" (231). As he does with the child's question "What is the grass?" in Section 6 (192), he again offers a set of provisional answers from Section 39 to the end of the poem, which amounts to a theory of the human self as a process rather than a definite object or specifiable state of being. The poet gives voice to what is best read as the paradigm of selfhood, "myself" (which can only speak in the first person after all), or the human body fully charged with the experience of the soul. "Behavior lawless as snow-flakes" (231), the self nevertheless contains a healing force that says to those who have yet to realize its full power, those lacking the sap of soulful life, "You there, impotent, loose in the knees, / Open your scarf'd chops till I blow grit within you" and "I dilate you with tremendous breath, I buoy you up" (Section 40, 232–3). Following a short catalogue of deities in Section 41 (including Jehovah, Osiris, Zeus, Buddha, and Allah, among others), the fully realized "myself" asserts the godliness of human life: "Accepting the rough deific sketches to fill out better in myself, bestowing them freely on each man and woman I see" (233). The ordinary becomes miraculous as common experience is deified – not only the human ("the mechanic's wife with her babe at her nipple interceding for every person born") but the animal as well: "The bull and the bug never worshipp'd half enough" (234). All appear in fully realized glory to the enlightened self, resulting in a vision that is at once democratic and ecological, each being filling a niche and contributing its integral part to the whole: "I do not call one greater and one smaller, / That which fills its period and place is equal to any" (238).

In Sections 46 and 47, the speaker in the first person directly addresses the second-person "you," another way of expressing the "flowing" quality of selfhood: "Not I, not any one else can travel that road for you, / You must travel it for yourself" (241). In this exchange, Whitman's "language experiment" engages two of the most unspecific words in English, "I" and "you," words that linguists call "deictics" or "shifters," whose referents cannot be found in the preceding text but only in the context of the utterance. Whitman specifies the "I" as "Walt Whitman" in Section 24 but then immediately proceeds to undermine the definiteness of the name by saying that "many long dumb voices" speak through him. Likewise, as seen in the variability of "you" in Section 5, the second-person pronoun is a free signifier specified only by context.

For Whitman, the pronouns offer a way to open the poem outward, creating connections beyond the limits of the text, and to express the self's tendency to lack stability, which becomes both a liability and a source of freedom. At times the clarity of the self is frightfully overwhelmed and must be reclaimed and reasserted. Yet because of this danger, selfhood is all the more an adventure for "myself" and "you." It is, as Whitman will say in a poem dating from 1856, "an open road," a journey he anticipates in his exchange with the indefinite "you" in "Song of Myself": "Shoulder your duds dear son, and I will mine, and let us hasten forth, / Wonderful cities and free nations we shall fetch as we go" (241). The poet offers a short catalogue at the end of Section 47 in celebration of the kinds of interlocutors ("you") that approach his ideal of selfhood ("closest to me") – the mechanic, the farm-boy, the soldier, the hunter, the "young mother and old mother" who "comprehend me" (243–4).

Sections 48–9 prepare for the hero's departure by showing the position of the self relative to the highest metaphysical states and conditions of being. Section 48 insists that "nothing, not God, is greater to one than one's self is" and urges readers not to lose sight of the self in theological speculation. "Be not curious about God," he says, "I hear and behold God in every object, yet understand God not in the least, / Nor do I understand who there can be more wonderful than myself" (244). Why should he want to see God, he wonders, when God appears in "faces of men and women I see" (245)? Having dispatched theology, Section 49 anticipates the objection that, unlike God, the self is limited by the boundaries of life and death. "And as to you Death, and you bitter hug of mortality, it is idle to try to alarm me" (245). Death becomes an "accoucheur," a midwife, whom Whitman addresses with the familiar "you." He likewise greets the vision of death embodied – "And as to you Corpse, / I think you are good manure" – and sees that the midwife death brings forth the living earth, which the poet gives a pleasing human form, suggesting the animated vitality and fertility of life that spreads identity in every direction: "I reach to the leafy lips, I reach to the polish'd breasts of melons." The stink of the corpse yields "the white roses sweet-scented and growing" (245).

In Sections 50 and 51, Whitman completes the transcendental sweep of the poem, dramatizing the poet at the edge of understanding, the limits of language. "There is that in me – I do not know what it is – but I know it is in me," he says of the force that he will at other moments call the soul (246). Now he is hesitant to name the "it," possibly for fear of contaminating it with theological and metaphysical prejudices of the reader. Having just claimed to "know what it is," he turns around and says, "I do not know it – it is without a name – it is a word unsaid, / It is not in any dictionary, utterance, symbol" (246). But he changes ground again and moves from negation to assertion of knowledge: "It is not chaos or death – it is form, union, plan – it is eternal life – it is Happiness" (246). Like Emerson, who says in "Self-Reliance" that "a foolish consistency is the hobgoblin of little minds,"[4] Whitman recognizes and here dramatizes the ultimate inadequacy of words and concepts to contain the fullness of being. "Do I contradict myself?" he famously asks in Section 51: "Very well then I contradict myself, / (I am large, I contain multitudes)" (246).

Called from his reveries by the "spotted hawk" that "complains of my gab and my loitering" in the finale of Section 52, the poet departs with the "last scud of day," drifting away with the clouds: "I effuse my flesh in eddies, and drift it in lacy jags" (247). He performs the words of his own funeral – "I bequeath myself to the dirt to grow from the grass I love" – the literal grass that contains the cells that were once his body and the figurative leaves of grass that are now his poetry and contain the written testament of his eternized being. "I stop somewhere," he promises, "waiting for you" (247), thus completing the poetic journey that begins with "I" and ends with "you."

Other poems dating from the 1855 *Leaves of Grass*

The other poems dating from 1855, all untitled in the first edition, include the two poems originally published in periodicals – the anti-slavery poem ultimately known as "A Boston Ballad" and the celebration of the revolutionary spirit of 1848, "Europe, the 72d and 73d Years of These States" – which advance the poetic agenda mainly by revealing the poet's political roots somewhat more explicitly than "Song of Myself." The other poems seem in form and theme to be spin-offs from "Song of Myself." They make use of free verse, catalogues of images, narrative vignettes, prophetic visions, direct address of the reader as "you," and the first-person persona "I" in varying modes. They also celebrate democracy, diversity, sexuality and the beauty of the body, the fecundity and power of nature, and the depth and range of the human soul in space and time. "A Song of Occupations," the second untitled poem in the first *Leaves*, brings Whitman's identity with the working classes into the foreground and also, in lines removed after 1855, offers a brief excursus on his attempt to create intimacy with the reader and simulate oral performance in the printed "voice." "Push close my lovers and take the best I possess," he says, "I was chilled with the cold types and cylinder and wet paper between us" (89). "I Sing the Body Electric" provides a focused treatment of sex and the body and sets in motion Whitman's meditations on gender difference that will by 1860 lead to his creation of separate groups of poems devoted to the love of man for woman ("Children of Adam") and the love of man for man ("Calamus"). "I Sing the Body Electric" clarifies the political dimensions of sexuality in the separate sections on "A man's body at auction" and "A woman's body at auction" (255–6), and thereby aligns Whitman with the dual causes of the social purity movement, the protests against slavery and prostitution (see Chapter 2). "There Was a Child Went Forth," in drawing upon childhood recollections, anticipates the way Whitman mythologizes the primal family and the process of growing up in the masterpiece of the 1860 edition, "Out of the Cradle Endlessly Rocking." "Faces" experiments with a thematically focused catalogue that suggests another step in the evolution toward his mature imagistic poetry of the postwar years.

One poem stands out as a particularly distinguished performance – "The Sleepers," the fourth untitled poem in the 1855 edition. "The Sleepers" shares much with "Song of Myself" – especially in style – but anticipates the poet's tendency in later editions to sharpen the thematic focus and stick to a single genre or mode of poetic expression within each poem. A more tightly unified example of the dream-vision genre, it stands as a night-time companion to the more day-lit "Song of Myself." Of all the 1855 poems, it most effectively reveals the anxiety that broods just below the surface of the "healthy-minded" optimism of the first edition of *Leaves*, exploring the dark side of human nature and the more psychologically threatening aspects of "the merge."

The first-person persona of "The Sleepers" is more consistently associated with the shamanic consciousness – the healer of the nation's nightmares – and more thoroughly concerned with spiritual transformation and the journey of enlightenment. A new twist on the vision of sympathetic imagination, the poem begins, "I wander all night in my vision" (542), proceeds through a communal dreamscape in which the shaman-poet enters into something like a trance state that allows him to observe and participate in the dreams of others, and closes with daybreak and awakening, literal and figurative enlightenment. He explains the main narrative premise of the poem thus: "I go from bedside to bedside, I sleep close with the other sleepers each in turn, / I dream in my dream all the dreams of the other dreamers" (543). The process disturbs the certainty of identity, leaving him "wandering and confused, lost to myself, ill-assorted, contradictory" (542).

The sleepers range in attitude from well-settled – "The married couple sleep calmly in their bed," "The men sleep lovingly side by side in theirs, / And the mother sleeps with her little child carefully wrapt" (543) – to the uneasy and profoundly disturbed: "the wretched features of ennuyés, the white features of corpses, the livid faces of drunkards, the sick-gray faces of onanists, / The gash'd bodies on battle-fields, the insane in their strong-door'd rooms" (542). The catalogue of sleeping faces indicates Whitman's interest in the science of the mind, such as it was in his day. The inner condition of the mind and spirit is revealed in the outward expression of the countenance, a concept also applied in the poem "Faces" that recalls his readings in phrenology and other eclectic medical sciences, as does his worry over the "secret sins" of alcoholism and "onanism" (masturbation).

The shamanic speaker takes the role of the healer – "I pass my hands soothingly to and fro a few inches from them, / The restless sink in their beds, they fitfully sleep" (543) – but in the process involves himself empathetically. The dreams claim him. The "fitfulness" of the troubled sleepers becomes a "fit" of sympathetic vision: "I am a dance – play up there! the fit is whirling me fast!" (543). He finds himself in the company of "nimble ghosts" that, like the shadowy figures in Section 28 of "Song of Myself," suggest half-formed fantasy figures or even elements of the poet's own personality, various faculties of his psychological make-up. "Well do they do their jobs those journeymen divine," he says, using the name for free workingmen who go from job to job without corporate affiliation. "I reckon I am their boss," he says, "and they make me a pet besides," a figure of both power and affection. The journeymen awaken the sexual desire of the boss/pet. They "lift their cunning covers to signify me with stretch'd arms," drawing him into their "gay gang of blackguards" with "mirth-shouting music and wild-flapping pennants of joy" (544). The word "gay" was not yet a slang term for homosexuality in Whitman's day, but worries over "onanism" in the public discussion of young men's sexual development may have been rooted in an emerging homophobia that would look upon mutual masturbation as subversive of a rigidifying heterosexual norm. Middle-class anxiety over the danger of contact of young men with the working classes, represented here by the journeymen, may also have arisen from the fear of homosexual initiation or exposure to a wildly indiscriminate sexual appetite that was thought to have raged among men who worked primarily with their bodies. The parade of fantasy figures, blackguards (literally users of foul language) with their phallic "pennants of joy," and the mention of "cunning covers" lifted secretly in the night suggest the homoeroticism of Whitman's dreamscape and hint at his particular sympathy with the dreaming onanist.

The dream vision shares with "Song of Myself" the trans-gendering and in general metaphoric transfiguring (queering) of the sexual act, which is also treated in "The Sleepers" as an analogue for the mystical experience. At the end of the poem's second section, the poet says, "I am she who adorn'd herself and folded her hair expectantly, / My truant lover has come, and it is dark," then addresses the night directly, "Double yourself and receive me darkness, / Receive me and my lover too" (544). The darkness itself becomes a metaphorical lover, to whom the poet croons, "Darkness, you are gentler than my lover, his flesh was sweaty and panting, / I feel the hot moisture yet that he left me" (544). As the vision dissipates, the feminine persona makes her exit – "I fade away" (544) – and leaves the speaker with the post-coital calm that, as in "Song of Myself," suggests the arrival at the mystical state of fulfillment and unity with all being. With "my sinews . . . flaccid," he says, "I descend my western course," like the sun (545).

His journey presents the speaker with a number of scenes and vignettes, in all of which he seems to have a peripheral role, although the story occasionally absorbs him, as in dreams in which the roles of viewer and participant are confused or overlapping. In the reportorial mode, he witnesses a "beautiful gigantic swimmer" dashed against the rocks of the sea and killed (545–6). In the epic mode, he narrates the defeat of Washington's troops at the Battle of Brooklyn and tells how after the battle the general greets his troops: "The chief encircles their necks with his arm and . . . kisses lightly the wet cheeks one after another" (547). He tells a family story, how his mother in her youth was visited by a Native American woman whose "wonderful beauty and purity" made the white girl long for another visit, which never happened (547). The swimmer, the general, and the mother in her youth variously represent the experience of personal loss, with the poet giving vent to the elegiac strain that he would powerfully realize in poems published in the 1860s.

In "The Sleepers," the poet is intent on resolving the sense of loss, on rising with the sun at the end of the poem healed and restored by the descent into darkness and exposure to the fearful side of his fantasies. The turn occurs at the beginning of Section 7 with the morning's "show of the summer softness" and the "amour of the light and air" that draws the poet out of the "Autumn and winter . . . in the dreams" (548). To compensate for the suddenness of the resolution (which may well seem too fast, and thus forced or artificial, to some readers), Whitman employs a technique that later becomes a staple in his poetic repertoire – the reprise.[5] As in musical performances in which the themes of key songs or movements of the work are briefly recounted at the end, the various actors and scenes of the poem are reviewed – "The beautiful lost swimmer, the ennuyé, the onanist, the female that loves unrequited, the money-maker" (548) – and brought together into thematic unity to advance the poem's ultimate aim, in this case, to reiterate the healing vision of the soul's, the body's, and the nation's beauty. Having "trusted himself to the night," as he says in Section 8 (550), he will all but inevitably "rise betimes" (551).

1856: poems of sexuality and the body

Little more than a year had passed since the publication of the first edition when Whitman brought out the second edition of *Leaves of Grass* in 1856. Not surprisingly, he continued to develop many of the themes and techniques set in motion in 1855. Chief among these was the emphasis on sexuality and the body.

The poem ultimately named "Spontaneous Me" insists on the continuity of the individual's sexual desire with all the creative forces of nature. More vigorously even than in "Song of Myself," Whitman connects the procreative drive with the artistic impulse – the penis becomes the "poem drooping shy and unseen that I always carry, and that all men carry" (260). He also associates sex figuratively with the nutritive acts of natural creatures, such as the "hairy wild-bee that murmurs and hankers up and down, that gripes the full-grown lady-flower, curves upon her with amorous firm legs, takes his will of her, and holds himself tremulous and tight till he is satisfied" (261). Informed by Whitman's erotic vision, the world undergoes a metaphorical transformation. In treating sexual desire and activity as universal and natural, Whitman follows the sex reformers and phrenologists of his day, one group of whom had signed on as his publishing agents in 1856. Like the authors of the social purity literature, he seems to have in mind an audience of young and men on the verge of sexual awakening, the "young man that flushes and flushes, and the young woman that flushes and flushes" (261). Yet in "Spontaneous Me," Whitman leaves the sex educators behind in an outright celebration of masturbation, offering rare insight into the hidden practices that begin in adolescence – "The young man that wakes deep at night, the hot hand seeking to repress what would master him" – but that continue into adulthood (261). Contrary to the typical advice in the sex manuals, which warned of insanity or worse, and inverting the negative image of "the sick-gray faces of onanists" in "The Sleepers" (542), in this poem Whitman makes a hero of the onanist, the preferred euphemism for the masturbator in nineteenth-century society, a term alluding to the biblical figure of Onan, condemned by God for spilling his seed upon the ground (Genesis 38.8–10). The poem's speaker models an unashamed release of the "limpid liquid" whose "vex'd corrosion so pensive and so painful" produces a "torment" of incomplete desire, "an irritable tide that will not be at rest" (261). The hero gives voice to the natural man, the "spontaneous me" liberated from the conventions of repression – "The souse upon me of my lover the sea, as I lie willing and naked" (262). He brings forth with studied nonchalance "this bunch pluck'd at random from myself" – literally a handful of semen, figuratively the poem itself: "It has done its work – I toss it carelessly to fall where it may" (262). "Spontaneous Me" was initially called the "Bunch Poem," in reference to the seminal seed as here described.

This radical poetic version of the common prose genre in Victorian America – the "talk to young men" – finds its feminine counterpart in the 1856 poem finally titled "A Woman Waits for Me." The poem draws upon the spirit of the most energetic women reformers of the nineteenth century, notably echoing Frances Wright, in its advocacy of a physically active and passionate womanhood. "Without shame the man I like knows and avows the delicious-ness of his sex," says the poet, "Without shame the woman I like knows and avows hers" (259). In an age when there were no female athletes, Whitman's ideal women "know how to swim, row, ride, wrestle, shoot, run, strike, retreat, advance, resist, defend themselves, / They are ultimate in their own right – they are calm, clear, well-possess'd of themselves" (259). The egalitarian message is undercut, however, by the insistent machismo of the speaker who declares that "all were lacking if . . . the moisture of the right man were lacking" (258). For all her strength and ability, the woman is finally reduced to a vehicle for the man's procreative purposes: "I dare not withdraw till I deposit what has so long accumulated within me" (259). The image of masculinity projected by the poem betrays as well a disturbing element of violence: "I do not hurt you any more than is necessary for you" (259).

"A Woman Waits for Me" has been singled out time and again as the most offensive of Whitman's writings – both in his own day and in later criticism. It was among the poems that may have led the phrenologists Fowler and Wells to drop *Leaves of Grass* from their publication list after 1856 and that prompted Emerson's advice in the late fifties for Whitman to cut certain poems in the name of good taste and good marketing. The poem was named by the Boston District Attorney who sought to ban Whitman's book in the 1880s. And it certainly does not stand up to the scrutiny of feminist and gender criticism in our own time. Finally, it offers a key example of one of the most interesting developments of Whitman's sexual poetics, the tendency of the image of womanhood to suffer when the poet formally separates it as a counterpart of manhood. Even a poem such as the 1856 "Unfolded Out of the Folds," which advances the overall program of Whitman's poetry of the body by balancing the phallic emphasis of "Spontaneous Me" and celebrating creativity with bold figures of the female genitalia, seems finally to single out maternity as the great glory of womanhood. A more varied portrayal seems beyond his reach. So long as "the merge" dominates his poetic consciousness, the feminine fares well, but as Whitman buys in more and more to the medical model of sexuality and the social notion of "separate spheres" – as his vision becomes hetero- or homosexual rather than generally erotic or broadly "queer" – woman is reduced, as D. H. Lawrence famously said, to a "great function – no more."[6]

1856: poems of the earth

Another of the "scientific" strains that deepened in 1856 might well be called ecological (although the term itself would not be coined until 1870 by the German scientist Ernest Haeckel). In poems like "Spontaneous Me," Whitman continued to develop the image of the Romantic hero confidently at one with nature, the figure who had greeted the "voluptuous cool-breath'd earth" in "Song of Myself" with the words, "Smile, for your lover comes" (208). But in other new poems, the relationship with the earth is rendered more prob-lematical and complex in ways that anticipate the growth of the conservation movement later in the century (the founding of the Sierra Club, for example, by John Muir in 1892, the year of Whitman's death). Whitman begins to question the ability of even the most sympathetic human consciousness to absorb and understand the mysteries of the earth.

Chief among the poems in this new vein is "This Compost." The poem begins on an ominous note: "Something startles me where I thought I was safest" (495). Disgusted by the thing he sees, the poet is suddenly alienated from the woods and pastures where he usually walks and from the sea where he swims. He never specifies what this "something" is, but leaves it unnamed, as if no word could capture its inhuman disgust. Very likely it is a corpse or a creature diseased and deformed. "O how can it be that the ground itself does not sicken?" he wonders, the significance of the thing extending beyond the momentary encounter: "Is not every continent work'd over and over with sour dead?" The earth comes to seem suspect and secretive, the withholder of death and disease, whom the poet addresses accusingly: "Where have you disposed of their carcasses? . . . Where have you drawn off all the foul liquid and meat?" (495). Acts that he had innocently pursued before this awakening he now encounters with a kind of gothic horror, an anxiety over some lurking indicator of destruction and decay: "I will run a furrow with my plough, I will press my spade through the sod and turn it up underneath, / I am sure I shall expose some of the foul meat" (495).

But the horror is not revealed in this little drama. Instead the poet exposes the rich soil of the fertile earth. "Behold this compost! behold it well!" he says, as if to himself. Although "every mite has once form'd part of a sick person," now only good things pour forth, which he enumerates in a catalogue of images: grass, beans, onions, apples, wheat, and the animals nurtured by the vegetative plenty, the birds, the cows, the poultry, the colt (495–6). "What chemistry!" he exclaims, "That the winds are really not infectious, / . . . That it is safe to allow [the sea] to lick my naked body all over with its tongues" (496). A kind of poetic chemistry thus becomes possible when the power of the earth's material chemistry is fully realized. The poet now restores the personification of the earth as lover that had been upset by the encounter with the disturbing "something" in the poem's early lines, which led him to avow, "I will not touch my flesh to the earth as to other flesh to renew me" (495). The drama of the lover's quarrel is resolved much as the darkness of the dream vision in "The Sleepers" is resolved. But in "This Compost," the resolution is accompanied by a new awareness of the earth's complexity and depth. The once-easy identifications and personifications yield to a respectful awe: "Now I am terrified at the Earth" (496).

Whitman pursues his skepticism over the human capacity to know and master the earth in the poem now known by the title "A Song of the Rolling Earth." Here he questions the confident attitude of his Romantic and scientific predecessors who believe that the objects and processes of the earth can be read like a book. Nature is not merely a set of signs patiently awaiting human interpretation, he suggests. Rather the earth has its own language – not "those upright lines . . . curves, angles, and dots" that we call words, but "the substantial words" that "are in the ground and sea" (362–3). This "language" is understood not by the human mind but only by the body. Indeed like the elemental states of "Air, soil, water, fire," "Human bodies are words" unto themselves that share in the language of the earth (363). "The earth does not withhold, it is generous enough," the poet says, but neither does the earth argue; it does not "scream, haste, persuade, threaten, promise" (364). In all, the earth remains, paradoxically, "the eloquent dumb great mother" (364). We look upon her indirectly, "her ample back towards every beholder, / . . . Holding up in her hand what has the character of a mirror, while her eyes glance back from it" (365). The earth can finally be known not by human words – "I swear I begin to see little or nothing in audible words" (367) – but in a soulful attitude that takes on the character of the earth itself, calm, still, silent (367). "No reasoning, no proof" can establish the reality of either the earth or the human soul (367). They cannot be known second-hand, but only through experience. At best, the soul can "echo" the earth, Whitman suggests in the poem's somewhat garbled ending. It is as if the poet, having discoursed on the limits on human language, dramatizes those limits in a reprise at the end of the poem that fails to resolve the main themes clearly.

1856: "Crossing Brooklyn Ferry"

The poem that shines out among the new poems produced for the second edition of *Leaves* is "Sun-Down Poem," later known as "Crossing Brooklyn Ferry." Like the ecological poems of 1856, it develops a rich imagery and far-reaching philosophy out of the poet's meditations on the human relation to place and a more specific celebration of his own most familiar home places. Instead of the countryside, which figures so powerfully in "This Compost," as well as "Spontaneous Me," "Crossing Brooklyn Ferry" portrays a symbolic cityscape out of his loving attention to the people, objects, and processes of the teeming metropolises that he called home, Brooklyn and Manhattan. Had he written no other poem celebrating the city, this one alone would justify Whitman's claim to the title of the New World's first urban poet.

Beginning with a joyful celebration of the masses returning home from work at sundown on the Fulton Ferry across the East River from Manhattan to Brooklyn – "Crowds of men and women attired in the usual costumes, how curious you are to me!" (308) – the poem does not rest in the joy of the immediate and the material. For one thing, it naturalizes the city from the very start, animating the currents in the river that move with the tides of the great ocean just beyond. In the opening lines – "FLOOD-TIDE below me! I see you face to face! / Clouds of the west – sun there half an hour high – I see you also face to face" (307) – the objects and processes of nature are lightly personified ("face to face") and the movement of people is anticipated, both the particular people of New York in 1856, and the people who shall cross the rivers and watch the sunsets of the future: "And you that shall cross from shore to shore years hence are more to me, and more to my meditations, than you might suppose" (308).

Readers of the future thus become the intended audience of this poem, the "you" whom the poet addresses directly. This kind of extended apostrophe is a rhetorical device used from 1855 on but employed especially often in the 1856 poems, not only here in "Brooklyn Ferry" but also in "Song of the Open Road," a kind of companion poem both in style and in its celebration of mobility and freedom from constraints. The constraints with which the poet deals most directly in "Open Road" are material and political, however, while in "Brooklyn Ferry" they are more philosophical and spiritual – the concepts of space and time, which Kant and other philosophers in the Western tradition considered to be the very foundations of human reason. Whitman's meditations on his future readers lead him in a different direction. "It avails not, " he concludes, "time nor place – distance avails not, / I am with you, you men and women of a generation, or ever so many generations hence" (308). His answer to the question he poses – "What is it then between us?" (310) – is not time or distance, "the scores or hundreds of years" (310), but rather the shared experience of sunset and the passage between the cities, and the crossing of rivers, all of which are touched lightly by the poet's sense of the symbolic, the significance of passing and movement: "Just as you feel when you look on the river and sky, so I felt, / Just as any of you is one of a living crowd, I was one of a crowd" (309). The very things that make human life transient and as changeable as the movement of water on the earth, the poems suggests – the sensual experience of beauty and the daily material contact with other people – are the very things that tie us to future generations of people.

This shared experience makes humanity, if not eternal, certainly durable well beyond the short space of a single lifetime. The eternal return of the generations is represented by the cycle of the tides. Much as the earlier Romantic poet Shelley had taken comfort in the cycle of the seasons, musing that "If winter comes, can spring be far behind" in "Ode to the West Wind," so Whitman finds joy in the tidal river's ebb and flow. The return of the flood tide carries the ferry eastward away from the setting sun, suggesting the life of the human race beyond the single sundown or death of the individual. A myth-making impulse emerges from such lines as "I too many and many a time cross'd the river of old" (309). The East River of nineteenth-century New York becomes "the river of old," across which every soul must take passage.

Images of light also figure symbolically. The many senses of illumination all play out in the poem, which dramatizes the experience of enlightenment as a dawning of understanding all the more poignant for its sundown setting. The outlines of light around the sea-gulls and people on the ferry (the "gods . . . that clasp me by the hand" [312]) make them appear as enlightened beings, figures in a holy drama. The poet describes his own reflection in the churning waters of the river in a manner suggesting the image of a haloed saint: "the fine centrifugal spokes of light round the shape of my head in the sunlit water" (309). The very absences of light, "the dark patches" in the scene on the water, signify human communion and connection. We are connected by the experience of evil, doubt, and guilt, he suggests in a famous confessional passage: "The dark threw its patches down upon me also / . . . I am he who knew what it was to be evil" (311). But the tenses of the verbs here suggest the ultimate victory of the light over the dark. The darkness of evil has been overcome. The "healthymindedness" of the poem prevails as the final sections reprise the scenes of illumination and turn from past to future.

"Brooklyn Ferry" is perhaps the most symbolic poem in the first two editions of *Leaves of Grass* and the most philosophically unified of the great cosmic dramas. But the thoughtfulness of the poem, impressive as it is, does not finally account for its enduring excellence. It is rather the poetic language that carries the day, the subtle play of symbolism and the striking images – "the vapor as it flew in fleeces tinged with violet" (309), the "scallop-edged waves in the twilight, the ladled cups, the frolicsome crests and glistening" (309), the sight of "mast-hemm'd Manhattan" (312), to name only a few. The objects captured in these fine images become for Whitman "dumb, beautiful ministers" that hint at the presence and continuity of the world's soul (313).

1860: Sea-Drift poems

In the 1860 (third) edition of *Leaves of Grass*, Whitman expanded key themes and techniques in a new outpouring of poems, along with revisions, new titles, and different arrangements of old poems. He continued to experiment with dramatizing the journey of selfhood in such new works as "Starting from Paumanok," "As I Ebb'd with the Ocean of Life," "Out of the Cradle Endlessly Rocking," and "Calamus" (all except for the latter known by different titles in 1860). While some poems remained rather long, others began to appear as short works arranged in thematic groupings or "clusters," as Whitman called them. In addition, with the war looming on the horizon and Whitman's personal problems mounting, the political exuberance of the earlier editions, and the frenetic optimism, yielded to a darkly brooding introspection in many of the new poems.

Nowhere is this psychological turn clearer than in "As I Ebb'd with the Ocean of Life" and "Out of the Cradle Endlessly Rocking," the two poems that dominate what would become the "Sea-Drift" cluster in the final arrangement of *Leaves*. Like the new overture poem for the 1860 volume, "Starting from Paumanok" (which uses the old Native American name for Long Island), the Sea-Drift poems invoke the place of Whitman's origins, the Atlantic shoreline with its headlands and beaches. The return to origins signifies the poet's interest in introspection, an inquiry into his values and motives, an effort to revitalize his waning inspiration and confidence, and a pilgrimage of spiritual renewal.

"As I Ebb'd" forms a kind of counterweight to "Crossing Brooklyn Ferry." The flood-tide of joyous certainty about the future in the 1856 poem yields to depression and doubt, associated with the ebb tide, in the 1860 poem. The poet feels that he is "Held by this electric self out of the pride of which I utter poems" (394). The "electricity" of the self – a metaphor for sexual arousal in such poems as "I Sing the Body Electric" – suggests the sense of irritability in "As I Ebb'd," the self charged with desire but finding no outlet, no means of release and expression. He stands on the "rim" of existence, the great ocean, amidst the "Chaff, straw, splinters of wood, weeds, and the sea-gluten" washed up by the waves, confronting his own self-doubt and insignificance (394). As the ocean rolls toward him with its awesome power, he muses, "I too but signify at the utmost a little wash'd-up drift," and for a moment he allows himself to regret "that I have dared to open my mouth": "Aware now that amid all that blab whose echoes recoil upon me that I have not once had the least idea who or what I am, / But that before all my arrogant poems the real Me stands yet untouch'd, untold, altogether unreach'd" (395). Self-doubt leads to a broader skepticism. Nature arises "to dart upon me and sting me, / Because I have dared to open my mouth to sing at all" (395).

Seeking some grounding for a deeper and truer understanding and expression of the self, the poet imagines a kind of primal family in the scene of his pilgrimage. The "ocean of life" becomes the "fierce old mother"; the island itself becomes the breast of the father upon which the poet throws himself to beg for mercy and understanding: "Kiss me my father, / . . . Breathe to me while I hold you close the secret of the murmuring I envy" (396). Lying thus, in the drifted jetsam of the low tide, the island offering its sandy breast, the ocean lapping at his feet, barely acknowledging (in a parenthetical aside) that "the flow will return," the poet yields entirely to the experience of life's ebbing, its loneliness and uncertainty. In this extreme state, he conveys more fully than anywhere else in *Leaves of Grass* the attitude that drives people to call upon a heavenly God: "You up there walking or sitting, / Whoever you are, we too lie in drifts at your feet" (396).

The all but desperate attitude of reaching for an audience the way a drowning person reaches for a lifeline occurs at many levels. In the characteristic Whitmanian versions of apostrophe, the poet calls out to nature (as a surrogate mother and father), to God (the ultimate Audience), and to the reader (the hope for future understanding in the absence of present companionship). This kind of heartrending appeal defines the poetic center of the new poems in the 1860 *Leaves*. It is a poetry predicated on loneliness and loss.

These motives produce spectacular results in the other major Sea-Drift poem, the spiritual autobiography ultimately titled "Out of the Cradle Endlessly Rocking," which critical opinion has enshrined with such works as "Song of Myself," "The Sleepers," "Crossing Brooklyn Ferry," and "When Lilacs Last in the Dooryard Bloom'd" as one of Whitman's most enduring masterpieces. More than the other major poems, all of which fall roughly in the category of "cosmic drama" or "ode of selfhood," "Out of the Cradle" features a rhapsodic narrative, a reminiscence of a key event in the poet's early life, most likely fabulous or mythic rather than strictly autobiographical. The story tells of how, as a boy, the poet habitually goes to the seaside to watch a nest of mockingbirds, male and female. The voice of the poem alternates between the poet's narration, presented in regular typeface, and a representation of the he-bird's song in italics. The song of the bird progresses from joy to panic to mourning as the story tells how the bird's mate fails to return to the nest one day. In realizing the beauty of the male bird's song, at every stage from joy to grief, the boy grows "ecstatic." With his "bare feet the waves, with his hair the atmosphere dallying," with "strange tears down the cheeks coursing" in deepest sympathy, he takes the bird as his "dusky demon and brother," and from the merging of impressions and the welling up of "the thousand responsive songs" within him, he discovers his vocation as a poet, the "chanter of pains and joys" (388): "My own songs awaked from that hour" (392–3).

Whitman carries his interest in symbolism and his experiments in poetic form to new heights in this poem, creating a wild landscape charged with psychological significance. The beach again represents a mental state situated between placid domesticity, the "fields" and the "bed" the boy leaves behind, and the primal source of life from which we all arise, the ocean as a "cradle endlessly rocking," its unflagging motion suggesting the continued possibility of birth and rebirth. The scene of the "mystic play of shadows twining and twisting as if they were alive" and "the yellow half-moon late-risen and swollen as with tears" (388) recalls the dreamscape of "The Sleepers" and anticipates the elegiac strains of "When Lilacs Last in the Dooryard Bloom'd." The landscape, alive with meaning, takes on human attributes and, thus personified, represents aspects of the poet's own being. The singing bird is the outward representation of his own poetic life; having once sung out of joy and hope (in the poems of 1855), he now sings out of sorrow over the loss of love (the death of his father in 1855 perhaps, the possible loss of a loving companion in the late 1850s, or the loss of the admiring readership he had once anticipated for his poems). The murmuring ocean is the outward symbol of the poet's mother-sense, his knowledge of the processes of nature by which the earth claims back the creatures to whom life is given. The awareness comes over him as the sea washes over a bather at its edge – an ecstatic, semi-erotic experience: "Creeping thence steadily up to my ears and laving me softly all over, / Death, death, death, death, death" (393).

Thus imbued with language and identity, the landscape "speaks." Or rather it sings. The poem is structured as an opera. "Hissing melodious," the voice of the sea joins the "aria" of bird song and the response of the "arous'd child's heart" (392–3). The chiming note of the fivefold "death" forms the underlying motif of a rhapsodic trio. The suggestion of the wave-like repetition is that the continuation of life requires the repeated confrontation with the awareness of death. Each loss means re-harmonizing the continuance of life with the steady throbbing of death-awareness.

"Out of the Cradle" is somewhat more "literary" than the poems of 1855 and 1856, more attuned to the history and conventions of Western artistic practice. In addition to modeling the poem upon the opera, Whitman draws freely upon books of natural history and echoes the works of other poets – most obviously, perhaps, the poetry of Tennyson and the most famous contemporary American poem that features a talking bird (though one far less articulate than Whitman's mockingbird), Edgar Allan Poe's "The Raven." Whitman had written in the 1855 Preface, "The poems distilled from other poems will probably pass away" (26), but by 1860, he had begun to realize that his most receptive audience was not the omnibus drivers and workingmen he befriended in Manhattan, but rather the literary Brahmins of Boston and the Bohemian circle of artists he met at Pfaff's Beer Cellar, who liked their poems nicely distilled. Indeed, the so-called "King of the Bohemians," Henry Clapp, published the first version of "Out of the Cradle" in an 1859 issue of his journal *The Saturday Press.*

With this poem, a subtle trend emerges in Whitman's work. He tended to be slightly more willing to bow to convention or to court a particular audience in poems that he published first in periodicals. The poems written exclusively for *Leaves of Grass* were always the more daringly experimental and iconoclastic. The first three editions, which contained a higher percentage of first-run poems, thus tended to be the most poetically revolutionary volumes. After 1860,

Whitman was more likely to try out the poems in newspapers or magazines before he included them in the newest edition of *Leaves*, using his increasing notoriety to exploit the burgeoning market for periodical poetry at the middle of the century.

1860: gendered clusters – "Children of Adam" and "Calamus"

Whitman's division of shorter poems into clusters seems to have begun with his composition of the twelve poems known collectively as "Live Oak, with Moss," the manuscript sequence that he revised into the "Calamus" cluster for the 1860 *Leaves*. "Live Oak" develops a definite narrative sequence describing the stages of the poet's progress from loving a man as a particular emotional experience to a more general kind of human love. He tells of his recognition that he cannot live alone and continue to write poetry. He proclaims his love for the man that absorbs all his attention and leads him to question his vocation as a singer of heroic songs. He confesses his pain at the ultimate separation from the lover. He recounts his adjustment thereafter, including musings about how his own emotional make-up compares to that of other men – "Is there even one other like me – distracted – his friend, his lover, lost to him?" He reveals his dream of "a city where all the men were like brothers." And in an interesting allusion to his frustrated ambition to become a schoolteacher, he announces his continuing search for "élèves," or students, most of whom are unlikely to suspect the volcanic intensity of his feelings toward them.[7]

The narrative thread of "Live Oak" is swamped in the final published version of "Calamus" by the inclusion of other poems that emphasize the political themes of brotherhood (such as "For You O Democracy"), the foundational experience of friendship ("The Base of All Metaphysics"), and the poetic relationship of poet to reader in a kind of allegory that relates falling in love to reading an appealing book (a trend best exemplified in the "Whoever You Are Holding Me Now in Hand" and "Are You the New Person Drawn toward Me?"). The 1860 "Calamus" group offers numbered poems suggesting a sequence that roughly follows the movement of "Live Oak" from particular to general, but in later editions Whitman dropped the numbers and used titles for the individual poems that further obscured the narrative momentum. The darker emotions of pain and loss are also muted, though they survive in the twining of love and death in poems like "Scented Herbage of My Breast," in several self-questioning moments that reveal doubts about the poet's previous heroic mission, and in the secretive tone that pervades the poems. In the introductory poem "In Paths

Untrodden," for example, Whitman mentions "the secret of my nights and days" (268). In "Whoever You Are Holding Me Now in Hand," he warns that "all is useless without that which you may guess at many times and not hit, that which I hinted at" (271). And in "Here the Frailest Leaves of Me," he says, "Here I shade and hide my thoughts, I myself do not expose them, / And yet they expose me more than all my other poems" (283).

The original story and the range of emotions in "Live Oak" disappear all but completely after Whitman excludes from the 1867 edition two poems that he had included in the 1860 *Leaves*: "Calamus 8" ("Long I thought that knowledge alone would suffice"), which renounces his poetic vocation to "sing" of heroes and "the grandeur of The States" in lieu of spending more time with his demanding lover; and "Calamus 9" ("Hours continuing long, sore and heavy-hearted"), which tells of his grief over the loss of the lover and wonders if other men ever feel the same. The sentiments of "Calamus 8" are voiced in a poem destined to remain in "Calamus" – the sonnet-like "When I Heard at the Close of the Day," in which the poet avows that his happiness derives not from "plaudits in the capitol" and the accomplishment of his former plans but in the joy of knowing that his lover is coming and will soon be "sleeping by me under the same cover in the cool night" (276–7). But the outright rejection of his former heroic motives no longer appears in the cluster. Certainly after the Civil War, he could not sustain his refusal to sing of heroic grandeur, and very likely, the elegiac emotions of his suffering over lost love came to seem trivial to him as well in light of the suffering and death he witnessed in the war.

"Calamus," with its celebration of "manly love," is matched with a cluster on the passionate love of man for woman, called "Enfans d'Adam" in 1860. Later changed to "Children of Adam," the cluster cobbles together poems from earlier editions, such as "A Woman Waits for Me" and "I Sing the Body Electric," with a few new poems, including "Once I Pass'd through a Populous City," which Whitman fitted out for "Enfans d'Adam" by altering a manuscript poem originally about the love of a man, changing the pronouns from masculine to feminine and the object of ephemeral love from a "rude and ignorant man" to "a woman I casually met."[8] Whitman's separation of the love of man from the desire for woman, which he designated with the phrenological terms of "adhesiveness" and "amativeness" respectively, represents a further step in the rationalist trend toward the categorization of sexual love into homo- and heteroeroticism.

Most critics agree that "Children of Adam" lacks the personal touch of "Calamus" as well as the far-ranging poetic implications, notably the allegory of writing and reading as acts of erotic love – a theme picked up by the striking poem at the end of the 1860 *Leaves*, "So Long." The best of the poems in

"Children of Adam," such as "Spontaneous Me," retain a more general treatment of sexual desire and instinct, a polymorphous eroticism that, though obviously shaped by the masculine experience, still forgoes a strict division of hetero- and homoerotic desire. Too many of the other "Adam" poems reproduce the aggressive image of masculinity and the reductive image of femininity that we encounter in "A Woman Waits for Me."

Chapter 4

Poetry after the Civil War

By the time the Civil War broke out in 1861, just after the publication of the third (1860) edition of *Leaves of Grass*, Whitman had discovered his poetic voice and established the major trends in writing that would absorb him for the rest of his career. After this point, according to the critical view that prevailed throughout most of the twentieth century, his work diminished in quality; he had done his best work during the burst of inspiration in the 1850s and produced only the occasional masterpiece thereafter. In recent years, this overarching narrative of his poetic development has been revised, if not abandoned. Critics have reevaluated the influence of the Civil War on Whitman's work (both the revisions of *Leaves of Grass* and the production of new poetry and prose), have taken a stronger interest in his wartime writings, and have advanced claims for a continued record of poetic excellence that reaches farther and farther into his later years.

This chapter takes the position that by 1860, Whitman had indeed reached a certain point of completion. He had developed the three poetic modes on which he would ultimately stake his reputation: the *cosmic/dramatic*, the *elegiac*, and the *imagistic*. Yet only in the cosmic/dramatic had he attained such a level of excellence that, had he written nothing else, he would still have left his signature indelibly upon American literary history. It remained for him to attain his full capacity as an elegiac and imagistic poet in his wartime and postwar poetry.

Accordingly, the main emphasis in this chapter falls upon the further development of the elegiac and imagistic modes in poems published after the war, with an occasional backward look to the roots of these developments in the prewar poetry. The chapter also considers two relatively minor poetic modes that can be identified at work over his entire career and that continued to develop after the war – occasional poems written to celebrate or promote particular historical events in history or the news, and poems that Whitman called "messenger leaves," which were addressed like speeches or letters to the reader, to characters he encountered either in actual experience or in imagination, and to natural and technological objects.

The term "modes" not only indicates poetic forms but also captures the etymological connections with "mood," suggesting the variety of emotional states invoked, and with "model," for all of Whitman's poems are, to some extent, an attempt to depict an outlook or a way of being in the world for prospective readers, every one of whom, in Whitman's view, stands as a potential participant in the poetic act. Any of the modes may dominate an individual poem, in which case, the poem belongs to a *genre* associated with the mode – a cosmic drama, an observational lyric, an elegy, an occasional poem, or a messenger poem. Or any mode may mix with the other modes, especially in longer poems like "Song of Myself." Each mode involves a characteristic tone and style and a typical set of themes:

- The *cosmic/dramatic mode* involves a celebratory tone and expansive style, with bursts of wild figurative language and what people in Whitman's day considered poetic "excess." Mainly concerned with the journey of selfhood, the overall trend is comic and affirmative, but may involve a dramatic movement away from a sense of alienation or isolation toward a sense of inclusion and immersion in society, nature, and the cosmos. "Song of Myself," "The Sleepers," "Crossing Brooklyn Ferry," and "This Compost" provide excellent examples from the early editions of *Leaves*. Some postwar poems, such as "Song of the Redwood-Tree" and "Passage to India," certainly contain elements of the cosmic drama, but this chapter argues that these two examples are better grouped under the headings of elegiac and occasional poems respectively.

- The *elegiac mode* appears in wartime poems explicitly dealing with the death of comrades (real or imagined). The mode proves dominant in *Drum-Taps* poems such as "Vigil Strange I Kept on the Field One Night" and the famous elegies on Lincoln. It is anticipated in such earlier works as "Out of the Cradle Endlessly Rocking," "As I Ebb'd with the Ocean of Life," and many of the "Calamus" poems, which invoke a deep and troubling sense of loss or alienation alongside a weaker sense of reconciliation than we find in the cosmic/dramatic poems (many of which contain elegiac sections or movements, notably "Song of Myself" and "The Sleepers"). The elegiac style tends to be expansive and the language highly figured, as in the cosmic dramas, but here we find a greater use of symbols, a broad operatic sweep to the drama, ritual echoes from the poetic tradition, and a more solemn tone.

The sense of bereavement and mourning deepens in the postwar poems to the point that it competes for dominance in the book as a whole with the optimistic "healthymindedness" that prevails in the cosmic dramas.

- The *imagistic mode* draws upon the powers of observation and description that Whitman also called upon as a journalist and memoirist. The image poems replace the visionary with the closely visual, the cosmic or global with the local observation, the expansive style with a more controlled manner and reportorial distance, resulting in a tone ranging from intense focus to a light, sometimes whimsical curiosity. Good examples appear in the enumerative catalogues of early poems like "Song of Myself" as well as in the scenic lyrics of *Drum-Taps* and such later short poems as "Sparkles from the Wheel" and "The Dalliance of the Eagles."

- The *occasional mode* appears most frequently as a kind of verse journalism in poems usually published first in the periodical press before they were incorporated into *Leaves of Grass*. Such poems appear in every edition, beginning in 1855 with "A Boston Ballad," but they increase in number in the postwar poems. They represent Whitman's efforts to keep his work current and in tune with the changing times. The most expansive example considered here is "Passage to India," which takes its cue from the technological accomplishments of modern industrial society.

- The *messenger mode* makes use of one of Whitman's favorite poetic techniques – apostrophe, or direct address. Like the occasional poems, messenger poems such as "To a Common Prostitute" and "You Felons on Trial in Courts" embody the poet's communicative motives, his efforts to connect his art and thought, and even his own person, to the people and events of his historical era. Such poems as "To a Stranger," "To You" and "So Long" show his desire to develop a poetics of intimacy with the readers of his work, while "To a Locomotive in Winter" and "To the Sun-set Breeze" show his use and transformation of the romantic genre usually known as the epistolary ode (which includes such famous examples as Shelley's "To a Skylark" and "Ode to the West Wind," Keats's "Ode to a Nightingale," and Poe's "To Helen").

It is important to remember that while Whitman tended to do his best work in the cosmic/dramatic mode in the 1850s, the elegiac in the 1860s, and the imagistic in poems from the Civil War and after, good examples of all three modes appear in every period. Likewise they intermingle in individual poems to produce unique poetic shades and tones. The modes suggest trends, not hard categories, though in the postwar work, the poems often suggest a more rigid adherence to a sense of genre.

Elegiac poems

Poems of the battlefield and war hospital

Whitman's brief visits to the scenes of battle and sustained encounters with wounded and dying soldiers as a volunteer in the Washington hospitals spurred and profoundly altered his poetic imagination, restoring his faith in the heart and soul of the common American and inspiring new forms of solemn, even reverent writing. To take an historical view, it is not an exaggeration to say that his experience in the war made him the greatest writer of elegiac verse in American literature. Psychologically speaking, the war enabled him effectively to convert the dark strain in his earlier poetry, notably the sense of loss and failure in the "Calamus" and "Sea-Drift" poems, into a powerful poetry of grief over the death of comrades and the cost of maintaining national unity.

In the *Drum-Taps* poems, first published independently and then incorporated as a cluster in *Leaves of Grass*, the best of the battlefield poetry in the elegiac mode is represented in "Vigil Strange I Kept on the Field One Night." Narrated in the first person, the poem is a dramatic monologue of a soldier who improvises a ritual by which to mourn a fallen comrade. It demonstrates a key purpose of the elegy – to memorialize not only particular people who have gone over into death but also the spirit that prevailed at the time of their loss. For Whitman, the spirit most worthy of memorial from the Civil War is devotion to the Union, not so much in the abstract political sense as in the personal sense realized among comrades in battle, something close to what he called "the merge" in the 1855 "Song of Myself" and "adhesiveness" in the 1860 "Calamus."

The poetic embodiment of memory involves an insistent repetition, both the frequent retelling of important incidents such as the death of comrades and the use of rhetorical devices often used to reinforce memory. Repetition works at several levels in "Vigil Strange." At the level of individual syllables and sounds, alliteration serves a vital role, both in phrases involving alliterative pairing, such as "swiftly slain," and across whole lines or passages – as with the "s" sound in "As onward silently stars aloft, eastward new ones upward stole" – a line whose formally parallel syntax also conveys a new kind of solemnity for Whitman (439). Whole words are also repeated for emphasis and to create a rhythmic thumping of a major theme. The best example in this poem is the word "vigil" itself, which is repeated twelve times, most often (in the technique known as anaphora) at the beginning of lines and parallel phrases: "Vigil for boy of responding kisses, (never again on earth responding,) / Vigil for comrade swiftly slain, vigil I never forget" (439). Whole phrases are repeated – either word for word or with a slight variation – to drive home particular emotional states, such as the speaker's sense of the finality of his loss. The phrase "boy of responding kisses, (never again on earth responding,)" is repeated twice without variation, for example, as are the phrases "never forget" and "not a tear," which hint that he is fighting to keep his emotion from overflowing both at the time of the vigil and in remembering it.

The impression created is that of a man going over and over the scene in memory, attending to the details of his story as ritually and as carefully as he had attended to the vigil itself and the interment of his friend. What is not repeated in the poem is also significant by contrast, suggesting a memory almost too painful to recall. The description of the actual burial, for example, is described only once, with spare language suggesting a crushing finality in the last two lines of the poem: "I rose from the chill ground and folded my soldier well in his blanket, / And buried him where he fell" (439).

Within this frame of the wartime elegy (as well as in his volunteer work in the hospitals), Whitman could vent fully his deep feelings for other men without too great a fear of violating conventional representations of friendship. In "Vigil Strange," the excess of love that the imagined speaker feels for his fallen comrade is suggested by familial language. The speaker calls the dead boy "my son and my comrade" (438). The speaker may possibly be the soldier's father. Fathers and sons could serve in the same armies of those days, when volunteers of all ages were accepted. If not, his love for the younger man verges on paternity, the same kind of love that Whitman felt for the young men he tended. Perhaps the best way to read the line is to say that the love he feels for the boy is so complete as to defy the available categories of fatherly and brotherly love, approaching the erotic. At the end of his vigil, he wraps the corpse in a blanket as a father might lay a child down to sleep, but puts him in the "chill ground" rather than in a warm bed (439). Thus in the elegiac poems of *Drum-Taps*, the sense of loss Whitman had expressed in the darker poems of "Calamus" finds an outlet that, if more socially acceptable, is also more devastating in its finality. Though he would continue to insist on the survival of the soul after death in these poems, the confident tone of earlier pronouncements about death, as in "Song of Myself" and "Crossing Brooklyn Ferry," is definitely attenuated.

Moreover, these poems leave Whitman less vulnerable to the charge of sentimentality. In the heyday of the New Criticism in the 1950s, which insisted that the best poems handle emotion with the distance and formality of the highest art, it was said that Whitman treated death sentimentally in poems like "Out of the Cradle." But sentimentality – what has been called "the commercialization of the inner self," a self-absorption that appeals to a similar self-centeredness in the reader – is transformed into a more profound Romanticism in Whitman's elegies: "a desperate effort to find in private resources an antidote and an alternative to the forces of modernizing society," in this case, the forces of modern war.[1]

Poems similar to "Vigil Strange," with imagined battlefield narrators compassionately witnessing scenes of death, include "As Toilsome I Wander'd Virginia's Woods," which tells of a soldier finding a rough grave marked with the words "*Bold, cautious, true, and my loving comrade*" (441), words that become a refrain in the poem (and that haunt the soldier's memory like a mantra of mourning). Another example is "A March in the Ranks Hard-Prest, and the Road Unknown." Here the poet draws upon his experience of the war hospitals in the image of one soldier attending to a mortally wounded comrade who dies looking into his eyes just before the order is given to march on. Some lines could be taken almost directly from Whitman's hospital diaries, such as "At my feet . . . a soldier, a mere lad, in danger of bleeding to death, (he is shot in the abdomen,) / I stanch the blood temporarily, (the youngster's face is white as a lily)" (440). The understated, almost reportorial language in such lines suggests a willful contraction of the emotions.

A more direct account of the hospital experience appears in "The Wound-Dresser." Here the poet imagines what account he will give of himself when as an old man young people will ask him about the war. He dismisses his first poetic response to the news of war, poems such as "Beat! Beat! Drums!" in which he greeted the outbreak of hostilities with a promotional fervor: "Arous'd and angry, I'd thought to beat the alarum, and urge relentless war, / But soon my fingers fail'd me"; instead, he says in "The Wound-Dresser," "I resign'd myself, / To sit by the wounded and soothe them, or silently watch the dead" (442–3). Now war becomes a matter not of struggle and glory on the field of battle – the "long march cover'd with sweat and dust" or the "shout in the rush of a successful charge" – but rather of the struggle of the body to live and adjust to injuries, illness, and death itself. In a virtual tour of a hospital ward drawn from memory, Whitman bears witness to the horrors of bullet wounds, gangrene, and diarrhea, of young men with death on their pallid faces, of the one who refuses to look at the stump that is left after amputation. He tells of the need to keep up a brave front and the tug of strong emotions: "These and more I dress with impassive hand, (yet deep in my breast a fire, a burning flame)" (445). And again, what remains through it all, as he says in the last lines of the poem, is the indelible compassion of one human being for another: "Many a soldier's loving arms about this neck have cross'd and rested, / Many a soldier's kiss dwells on these bearded lips" (445).

The *Drum-Taps* poems, perhaps more than any other English-language poems before those commemorating World War I, delve realistically into the psychology of war. "The Artilleryman's Vision," for example, tells of how a soldier at home relives again and again the scenes of war as his wife and baby lie sleeping. The poem attests to Whitman's awareness of the condition that would later be known variously as "battlefield fatigue" and "post-traumatic stress syndrome." Against the admitted reality of the trauma, the elegiac poems strain to rescue the love of comrades and the devotion that leads one man to die for another – emotions that Whitman felt, with an intensity renewed by the war, to be the foundation of hope for the success of the democratic experiment in the New World.

The Lincoln poems

In the death of Abraham Lincoln, Whitman discovered a poetic means by which to create a myth of the great comrade, the one whose loss could represent the loss of all the rest. Through the commemoration of Lincoln, the full sacrifice of those lost in the war could be memorialized. Just as the first-person persona of "Song of Myself" stands as the model for the great potential of the common American in the 1855 *Leaves of Grass*, so the figure of Lincoln comes to stand in Whitman's elegies for the great cost paid for the survival of the Union.

Whitman wrote four poems on the death of Lincoln – "When Lilacs Last in the Dooryard Bloom'd," "O Captain! My Captain!," "Hush'd Be the Camps To-Day," and "This Dust Was Once the Man" – which (with the exception of "This Dust") made up the *Sequel* to the 1865 *Drum-Taps* volume and which were ultimately included as the final poems of the "Drum-Taps" cluster in *Leaves*. The last two are quite brief. "Hush'd" contrasts the silent mourning of soldiers in camp on getting the news of the fallen leader with the former noise and confusion of battle. Whitman imagines the soldiers inviting him to break the solemn silence and "sing . . . in our name, / Sing of the love we bore him" (468). As in all these elegies, Whitman follows the universalizing tradition of the English elegy (from Milton on down) by withholding the name of Lincoln, suggesting the mythic stature of the dead leader. Everyone knows the one who is mourned; there is no need to name him. In addition, he is not one man only in death, but stands in the place of all who have died. "This Dust" celebrates the dead one as "Gentle, plain, just and resolute" – an ordinary man, but one "whose cautious hand . . . saved the Union of these States" (468).

"O Captain!" quickly became one of Whitman's best-known and most widely anthologized poems. Before he added it to *Sequel to Drum-Taps*, Whitman published the poem in the *Saturday Press*. The most conventional poem that

Whitman published after 1855 – with its regular stanza form, rhymes (albeit slant and irregular), and easily recognizable metaphors (Lincoln as the captain of the ship of state) – it is one of the best examples of Whitman's tendency to write more conventionally for the periodical audience. Whitman was asked so often to recite the poem in the years after the war that he ultimately grew sick of it. "Damn My Captain," he said to Horace Traubel, "I'm almost sorry I ever wrote the poem."[2] No doubt he was disappointed to discover that he was more likely to win the public favor he so desired by writing the very kind of formulaic literature that he had previously dismissed.

He might also have been disappointed that "O Captain!" was favored over the greatest of the Lincoln elegies, "When Lilacs Last in the Dooryard Bloom'd." As in the other Lincoln poems, Whitman draws upon the tradition of elegiac writing in English, but if he follows a formula in "Lilacs," it is primarily one that he devised himself in the 1860 poem "Out of the Cradle Endlessly Rocking." Both poems have the elegiac tone and operatic structure, the singing bird that is a "brother" to the poet (a thrush rather than a mockingbird in "Lilacs"), a setting near the shore of the US eastern seaboard (a swamp this time rather than a beach), and the poet returning to nature to mourn and to seek redemption and atonement. But the attitude of the two poems toward nature and death differs. The mood is more somber in "Lilacs," the release from the initial distress never complete. Whitman's experience of the war, his witness to the suffering and death of his fellow citizens followed by the assassination of President Lincoln, undermines his certainty that death "avails not" (as he said in the exuberant flood-tide poem "Crossing Brooklyn Ferry").

Like the ocean in "Out of the Cradle," the objects of nature represented in "Lilacs" speak of death to the poet, becoming symbols of his state of mind and signs of the historical changes underway – the great star "drooping" in the western sky, the dark cloud that threatens to hide the star, the lilac sending forth blossoms as if to resist the oppression of death and remind him of life, but finally becoming the token by which he vows to remember the President's death every time the spring returns. Unlike the mockingbird in "Out of the Cradle," whose very life seems to depend upon his mate, the thrush in "Lilacs" is a "hermit withdrawn to himself, avoiding the settlements," hiding away in "the swamp in secluded recesses" (459). The thrush is like the poet around the time of the national crisis, who by his own account hid away at the beginning of the war, going home to his mother's house in Brooklyn and writing on other topics, most of them dealing with the past. He was in Brooklyn again when the announcement came of Lincoln's assassination, having returned from Washington to recuperate from the strain of his work in the hospitals. The poet comes to identify with the bird, "the solitary singer," for in mourning Lincoln, he takes a mythic journey out of the settlements to the forest swamp to find his bearings in the face of death.

In tracing the path out of civilization and into the wilderness, the poem follows a roughly narrative structure. As in all his best poems, he fuses the poetic modes. Here he enlivens the elegy with elements of the cosmic drama, notably the mythic journey of self-discovery (or in this case, self-recovery, similar in form to "The Sleepers"). As the story begins, the flowers are blooming in the dooryard of an old farmhouse. The scene suggests a return (in memory or fantasy) to Whitman's childhood home on Long Island. From a bush of lilacs, the poet takes a sprig to toss upon the coffin of the dead President as the funeral train passes through the city on its famous circuit from Washington to Springfield, Illinois. In moving from the farmyard to the city where the coffin passes (an event Whitman did not actually witness, according to the biographers), the shift of setting in the poem follows the poet's own migration in his early manhood, replicating the pattern of Lincoln's life, too, as well as that of many thousands of young American men of the day who moved from the country to the city looking for work and a new kind of life.

The stateliness of the funeral procession depicted movingly in Section 6 – "the pomp of the inloop'd flags with the cities draped in black," the "mournful voices of the dirges pour'd around the coffin," the "dim-lit churches and the shuddering organs" (460) – and the improvised ritual of placing the lilac sprig on the coffin fail to satisfy the poet's need to atone and be redeemed from his sadness. The failure reminds him that his emotion arises not "for you, for one alone" – the dead leader – but for death itself. He then addresses "sane and sacred death" directly, telling of his desire to "cover you over with roses and early lilies" and copious sprigs of lilac – "For you and the coffins all of you O death." But the imaginative laying on of flowers also fails to provide the release he needs. As the night advances, "my soul in its trouble dissatisfied sank," and the drooping star, which he now calls comrade and which is identified with the fallen President translated into heavens in the manner of classical elegies and myths, "holds and detains" him (461–2).

The feeling of being held, the inability to break free from the compulsive return of thoughts about the dead comrade, drives the poet down the path to the swamp. In Section 10, he finds in the sea-winds the breath that he says he will make into a chant with which to "perfume the grave of him I love," thus augmenting the fragrance of the blossoms in his earlier offering, which failed to "cover over" death (462). Moving deeper into the dark woods, he imagines a "burial-house of him I love" which he adorns with "Pictures of growing spring and farms and homes, / . . . With floods of the yellow gold of the gorgeous, indolent, sinking sun, burning, expanding the air" and "With the fresh sweet herbage under foot, and the pale green leaves of the trees prolific" and "all the scenes of life and the workshops, and the workmen homeward returning" (462). The decorations of the death-house appear to represent the poems of his own book *Leaves of Grass*. In effect, he is in these lines dedicating his life's work, past and present, to the memory of the war and the dead President. Yet even this heartfelt dedication will not suffice.

The hint of what will ultimately release him sounds repeatedly throughout the poem in the song of the hermit thrush (appearing in the interludes of Sections 9 and 13), which continues to draw him toward the swamp. But still "the star holds me" and "the lilac with mastering odor holds me," he says (463). Not until Section 14 does he begin to find his way out of the cycle. Becoming aware of the "arching heavens of the afternoon swift passing" and the "many-moving sea-tides" – and the ordinary movements of the farm and city people – "the fields all busy with labor, / And the infinite separate houses, how they all went on, each with its meals and minutia of daily usages," he sees "enveloping" them all the cloud, "the long black trail," and with this vision, he says, "I knew death, its thought, and the sacred knowledge of death" (463–4). To indicate the closeness he feels to death, he personifies the knowledge of death and the thought of death as two comrades who take his hands and lead him to the thrush in the swamp.

The bird's song differs significantly from that of the mockingbird in "Out of the Cradle." Like the mockingbird's, the thrush's song has a regularity and a pattern of trilling repetition which distinguishes it from the "voice" of the poet (along with the use of italic type for the bird's song). Here, however, the tone is not agitated and intense, but soothing and calm, not only accepting of death, but inviting or invoking death much as Whitman invites the soul in "Song of Myself": "*Come lovely and soothing death*," sings the bird, "*Dark mother always gliding near with soft feet,* | *Have none chanted for thee a chant of fullest welcome?*" (464–5). The bird's acceptance of death signifies its integration in natural cycles that all creatures except humans seem not to question. The bird reminds the poet of his openness, the capacity to be transformed in the face of undeniable otherness, both human and natural. On this occasion, he must not only open himself to the word "death" but to the reality of death, which replaces the ocean as "mother" in this poem. In "Out of the Cradle," the mother-ocean spoke the word "death"; in "Lilacs," the mother is death itself. The poet's own spirit "tallies" with that of the bird, aligns with it, receives it, and is rewarded with a vision of death as "*deliveress*," a "*loving floating ocean*," a "*flood of . . . bliss*" (465). The vision brings the message that the suffering of war, though terrible, is over for those soldiers who have died, but not for the survivors, the sorrow of whom is drummed out with the relentless repetition of the word "suffer'd" in Section 16, the poem's finale.

With the vision, the cycle of grief is completed. With "death's outlet song," the remembrance of the ones who are beyond suffering, the grief can be released to flow into the death-ocean, and the poet can try to let go and return to the flow of life – "Passing the visions, passing the night, / Passing, unloosing the hold of my comrades' hands," he says in the closing stanzas of Section 16 (466). By comrades, he means primarily the personified abstractions, "the thought of death" and "the knowledge of death," but he also implies the release of the dead comrades of his visions whom he tries to leave to rest in peace, taking what comfort he can from the knowledge that in death their suffering is ended. The visions inspired by the bird's song show him that his obligation to the dead is fulfilled by his having shamanistically opened himself to the spirit of death, by having sung in his own voice, and by his vow to remember. The "fragrant pines" and the "cedars dusk and dim" provide the necessary perfume, the celebratory incense (467).

For all the beauty of the poem, which has been admired by critics from his own time down to the present, "Lilacs" failed to satisfy Whitman, who never named it among his greatest performances.[3] Perhaps he worried that in following so closely the patterns of an earlier poem ("Out of the Cradle"), he failed to do justice to the new poem's subject. Or perhaps he recognized the increasing conventionalism of his writing, even in poems like this one published first in book form and not for the magazine market. In addition to adhering closely to many of the conventions of the English elegy, for example, he also violates his own earlier poetic principles by personifying abstractions (the knowledge of death and the thought of death), a technique that he seems expressly to have forbidden to the ideal poetry described in the 1855 Preface.[4] Or perhaps nothing could satisfy his intense desire to keep the war fresh in the minds of the American people. Throughout his career Whitman returned again and again, in his prose writings and lectures, to the death of Lincoln, unable to find the resolution he seems dramatically to claim at the end of "Lilacs." He never stopped worrying that his fellow Americans had forgotten the struggle and the sacrifice exacted by the war.

Later elegiac writing

In the years following the war, Whitman continued to explore the poetry of death and loss in *Leaves of Grass*. Whole clusters of poems, such as "Whispers of Heavenly Death" and "Songs of Parting," were infused with the elegiac spirit. No doubt the drama of the war remained fresh in his mind for the rest of his life and prompted him to make elegy a central feature of his growing book.

Another influence was his own failing health and particularly the paralytic stroke that coincided with the death of his mother in 1873. Whitman looked back upon this profoundly disturbing time of his life in the 1881 poem "As at Thy Portals Also Death." One of his finest short elegies, the poem memorializes his mother much in the manner of his wartime poems. The memory of "the calm benignant face fresh and beautiful still" lying in her coffin stays with him: "I kiss and kiss convulsively again the sweet old lips, the cheeks, the closed eyes in the coffin." The image of the repeated kissing applies not only to the time of the funeral when the poet was moved "convulsively" (or compulsively) to sustain the last intimate contact for as long as he could, but also to the time thereafter when he would kiss her again in memory. The image of intimacy contrasts poignantly with the more formal language of eulogies in the poem – "the ideal woman, practical, spiritual, of all of earth, life, love, to me the best" – which reflects the virtual worship of maternity common in Whitman's day (the era in which "Mother's Day" was first declared an official holiday in the US and "the angel of the house" was the dominant archetype of femininity). That the first troubling signs of his own eventual death should appear at the same time as his mother's death seems to Whitman a portent of their never-ending connection, "the divine blending" (604).

Two poems written during his actual recovery from the 1873 stroke reveal both the intensity of the event and Whitman's late-career tendency to rework tried and true poetic patterns. "Prayer of Columbus" and "Song of the Redwood-Tree," both published first in *Harper's Magazine* in 1874, recall the pair of 1860 poems written during an earlier life crisis or cycle of depression – "As I Ebb'd with the Ocean of Life" and "Out of the Cradle Endlessly Rocking." Like "As I Ebb'd," the "batter'd, wreck'd old man" of the Columbus poem is cast to his knees on a "savage shore . . . along the island's edge" (540). Like "Out of the Cradle," the operatic redwood poem mingles the modes of cosmic drama and elegy and gives voice (in italic type) to a natural creature, this time not a bird but a tree.

Of the many differences in the two pairs of poems, the most striking is Whitman's attempt in the later poems to distance himself from his own suffering and emotions. Instead of writing in the first person, more or less performing himself, as he does in the 1860 poems (though the distancing begins with the song of the mockingbird), he dramatizes his own alienation and hurt in "Prayer of Columbus" by putting his own crisis into the mouth of the historical figure. As Columbus had, according to legend, discovered America, Whitman had discovered American poetics. Feeling neglected and failed by the time of his stroke and rapid aging in the postwar years, Whitman identifies with the figure of the discoverer whose contributions were underrated or misunderstood in his own day but grew to legendary proportions after his death. Columbus' vision at the end of the poem – of "Shadowy vast shapes" that "smile through the air and sky" and "anthems in new tongues I hear saluting me" (542) – is clearly Whitman's hope for the future success of his own life project.

The autobiographical element in "Song of the Redwood-Tree" is even more subtly disguised. As with the mockingbird in "Out of the Cradle," the redwood tree represents Whitman's lament for all that has been lost. The particular attitude that comes through this time, however, is resignation. The great tree greets the generation of advancing pioneers and woodcutters as a "superber race" and willingly accepts the ax (352). The poem begins and ends with the voice of the poet whose ears are especially attuned to the sound of the forest spirits leaving the trees – the dryads and hamadryads – voices unheard by the new generation of settlers. The tension between the assertion of the new generation's excellence and rightful claim to the land and the apparent insensitivity of that generation to the subtleties of spiritual nature is awkwardly resolved in favor of the woodcutters. By the end of the poem, the poet is celebrating in harmony with the now-fallen tree the "new society at last, proportionate to Nature" (354), as if society were not dependent upon the resources of the earth but itself an adequate replacement for nature. Thus in the vein of earlier poems that turn the cosmic drama to the service of promoting westward expansion – such as "Song of the Broad-Axe" (1856) and "Pioneers! O Pioneers!" (1865) – "Song of the Redwood-Tree" devolves into a promotion of the doctrine of manifest destiny, the concept that allowed white Europeans to sweep across the continent, transforming land and culture in the name of progress. Whitman's ill-sorted ambivalence over this outcome finds voice in the persistent elegiac tone that continues to echo beneath the incomplete reconciliation at the end of the poem.

That Whitman was uncomfortable with the direction that progress and democracy were taking after the war becomes much clearer in the prose works (discussed in Chapter 5). In *Leaves of Grass*, he seems intent upon preserving the initial vigor and forward-looking hopefulness that he first sounded in "Song of Myself." But in many of these postwar poems, the elegiac impulse threatens to color the entire performance with its darker tones.

The emergence of the image

From visionary to visual poetics

Vision in one form or another is an essential element in the poetic process as Whitman understood it throughout his career, but in poems written after 1860, the poet began gradually to leave behind what can be called the "visionary" aspects of his role – the seer as prophet – and to favor the more simply "visual" functions of a new poetic character: the seer as witness. The shift from visionary to visual poetics corresponds to a subtle shift away from Romanticism (or Victorianism) and toward realism (or modernism) in Whitman's work and in American literary history as a whole. The change of focus was also likely to have been influenced by the shift from orality to literacy in the culture at large. An age dominated by the public lecture and the Sunday sermon was giving way to the age of the penny press and dime novel even in the popular culture. As for the political culture, the best speeches of the day were no longer given once to a single audience gathered for some occasion. They were reprinted in newspapers and widely distributed. President Lincoln himself may have attempted to accommodate this cultural shift in his Gettysburg Address. The unprecedented brevity of this speech made it suitable for quick reading and comprehension and likely contributed to its elevation as the most famous presidential speech in American history.[5]

The first three editions of *Leaves* favor the oral exchange of information typical of a village or small-town culture, the values and immediacy of which the poet seems eager to carry over into print. The functions of voice and ear predominate. In large and expansive poems, the poet "sings" the songs of occupations, the rolling earth, the broad-ax, joys, and, most famously, himself. He listens to voices, liberates and transforms them. He hears America singing, the mockingbird trilling for a lost mate, the low and delicious word Death in the voice of the sea. He complains that the printing process comes between himself and the reader, and does all he can to approximate the face-to-face encounter of "you" and "myself." Visionary orality plays its greatest role in the cosmic dramas, in which the poet typically claims a transcendental view beyond the ordinary limits of present experience and gives voice to his expanded understanding for the benefit of his audience. In "Song of Myself," for example, Whitman imagines himself floating above the rooftops of the world, participating in historical events that occurred before he was born, and seeing through the eyes of women and slaves. In mystical moments of inspired clarity, he has healing visions of a world united in cosmic love. In "The Sleepers," the sympathetic imagination allows him to see into the bedrooms and even the dreams of his fellow citizens as they lie in their beds. The healing power of cosmic love promises to save the world from its restless slumbers. In "Crossing Brooklyn Ferry," his vision of deathless unity reaches across time and space to encompass future readers, whom the poet addresses directly with prophetic certainty. In all of these visions, somewhat ironically, the voice remains the primary force; the poet declares famously, "I sound my barbaric yawp over the roofs of the world" (247). He appears as "A call in the midst of the crowd, / My own voice, orotund sweeping and final" (234).

The same pattern of vocalized vision predominates in the more elegiac poems. In "Out of the Cradle Endlessly Rocking," he celebrates his vocation as a poet operatically as a dreamlike vision of childhood reminiscences, singing a trio with the forlorn mockingbird and the hissing ocean. In "When Lilacs Last in the Dooryard Bloom'd," the turbulent vision of the many who died in the war appears to the poet as he communes with the personified figures of death to achieve the release he needs to go forward in his poetic mission. Again, the singing of the bird signals the release. In "Song of the Redwood-Tree," the poet offers a grand vision of westward expansion undercut by a competing vision of a deforested, utterly transformed western landscape, the defeat of nature by society. The voice of the forest spirits cannot be heard over the sounds of the falling ax until the poet gives them voice. In "Prayer of Columbus," the old explorer talks to God and is rewarded with a vision of future glory. Visions, dreams, images from the past, insights into the future – these are the stuff of prophesy, another name for which is *visionary* (though prophesy traditionally proceeds by the power of the spoken word, which interprets the vision and carries it forth into the world).

Yet even as these visionary performances dominated his poetry, the visual element was starting to emerge. This other side of vision in Whitman's work appears early in the carefully crafted details of the great catalogues, images that contract into poignant still lives or expand into anecdotes and narrative vignettes. By the 1860s, Whitman began to take a special interest in developing visual poetry as a genre in its own right. No longer are the images necessarily connected to the big themes of self-discovery, diversity-within-oneness, natural abundance, and so on. Now they seem somehow to speak for themselves or to require no statement from the poet-commentator. They are no longer the text of a "song," celebratory oration, or sermon; the function of the poet is to serve as a witness or reporter.

The emergence of the image poem in the 1860 *Leaves* coincides with the doubts Whitman expresses over his poetic mission in such poems as "As I Ebb'd with the Ocean of Life." Here he refers to his previous work as "my arrogant poems" and "all that blab whose echoes recoil upon me" and wonders why he ever "dared to open my mouth to sing at all" (395). While such lines have led biographers and critics to the view that Whitman had fallen into a depression over the state of his work in general and its failure to attract a large and enthusiastic audience, few have noticed that he states his dissatisfaction in terms related to the sound of his voice – "blab," "echo," and the act of opening the mouth to sing. Quite likely, he was dissatisfied with a particular element of his work, and the sonic language used here hints that the offending element was the tone of voice that dominated the early editions of *Leaves of Grass*. Certainly he would continue to celebrate the power of the human voice (in such poems as "Vocalism," which dates from 1860) and to write in the oracular style of the cosmic drama, but generally speaking, Whitman seems to have grown tired of preaching; his oratorical ambitions, if not totally lost, were certainly diminished.

Another poem of the 1860 edition, "I Sit and Look Out," supports this reading. The poet reports a list of injustices that he witnesses – "all the sorrows of the world, and . . . all oppression and shame" (411) – as he looks upon the world through a window that at once allows him to see the problems and separates him from active participation. A brief catalogue follows that lists such figures as "young men at anguish with themselves," a "mother misused by her children," a "treacherous seducer of young women," "battle, pestilence, tyranny" – the sorts of problems that had prompted the shamanic narrator of "Song of Myself" and "The Sleepers" to offer songs of healing (411). He sees a "famine at sea" with "sailors casting lots who shall be kill'd to preserve the lives of the rest," which may, like the other images, have come from Whitman's reading of history or the news, but may also suggest an allegory for the nation on the eve of Civil War, the wrecked ship of state (a well-worn metaphor that he would later use later in "O Captain! My Captain!"). His watchful eye sees the privileged and the poor alike, the kind of characters whom he had addressed with indignation and sympathy in earlier poems. But now, with a resignation resulting perhaps from the his sense of war's inevitability, he steps back: "All these – all the meanness and agony without end I sitting look out upon, / See, hear, and am silent" (411).

After 1860, he continues to appeal to the value of silence in such poems as "When I Heard the Learn'd Astronomer." Here the poet declares, "When I sitting heard the astronomer where he lectured with much applause in the lecture-room, / How soon unaccountable I became tired and sick." Leaving the lecture hall, the poet goes out into the "mystical moist night-air" and looks up at the stars "in perfect silence" (409–10). In one sense, he seems to reject the calculative method of the scientist's "charts and diagrams" in favor of a more mystical and romantic communion with nature. But in another sense, he rejects the room filled with an audience applauding the lecture and favors instead the kind of silent solitude that favors not only mystical star-gazing but also reading and writing in privacy.

The silent response suggests a farewell to his old ways and a commitment to a new approach. It indicates an abandonment not of poetry so much as voice.

Now his goal is to use his eyes and invite the reader to do the same. The visual image may no longer work in support of visionary prophesy, but he could nevertheless take the performance of the visual to new heights.

The later imagist poems

At the farthest reach of the imagistic experiment is a poem like "The Runner," first published in the 1867 *Leaves*. It consists of only four lines with virtually no commentary:

> On a flat road runs the well-train'd runner,
> He is lean and sinewy with muscular legs,
> He is thinly clothed, he leans forward as he runs,
> With lightly closed fists and arms partially rais'd. (413)

In this poem, as in others of the same period, images lead the poet in new directions, sometimes leaving him content to have recorded the thing when before he might have offered a sermon or moral. "The Runner" might have appeared in a catalogue in "Song of Myself." Or it might have led the poet to a confessional utterance in the vein of "Calamus." Or he might have intensified the image with a religious analogue, as he did in the striking poem of *Drum-Taps*, "A Sight in Camp in the Daybreak Gray and Dim," in which he superimposes "the face of the Christ himself, / Dead and divine and brother of all" upon the face of a dead soldier – "a face nor child nor old, very calm, as of beautiful yellow-white ivory" (441). Or, as in another 1867 poem, "A Noiseless, Patient Spider," he might have gone the conventional route of offering a reflection on human striving. "A Noiseless, Patient Spider" begins with the observation of a spider isolated on a promontory. The poet watches as it launches forth "filament, filament, filament, out of itself, / Ever unreeling them, ever tirelessly speeding them," a process that in the second stanza he likens to the work of his own soul that, "in measureless oceans of space," casts about for an anchor hold (564). In allegorizing the spider, Whitman uses a technique well known in the preaching as well as in the nature writing of his day, using a natural object to moralize on human life (compare, for example, the famous poem "To a Waterfowl" by Williams Cullen Bryant or the equally famous "The Chambered Nautilus" by Oliver Wendell Holmes). By the second stanza, the poet leaves the natural object behind, opting for a moral about the tireless longing of the human soul.

Just as often, however, as the process of change unfolded in the 1860s, Whitman stops short of moralizing or sermonizing, as he does in "The Runner." He seems satisfied with the sufficiency of the thing before the eyes: "lightly closed fists and arms partially rais'd." Or he starts with a reflection on the human condition in the title or first line and then gives it up, letting the image stand without comment, as in the one-line poem of 1860, "To Old Age": "I see in you the estuary that enlarges and spreads itself grandly as it pours in the great sea" (414). The marshland image completes the thinking rather than beginning the kind of extended reflection we get in "A Noiseless, Patient Spider" that starts with the spider and ends up in "measureless oceans of space" (564). When the poems move toward the particular, rather than away from it toward abstraction, the images seem almost to absorb thought and resist the transcendental imagination and the Romanticism of the early poems.

In "Sparkles from the Wheel," a city poem of 1871, the poet stops with a group of children to watch a knife-grinder at work. As the old man bends to his work, Whitman joins the fascinated group of "attentive, quiet children" mesmerized by the "hoarse purr of the whirling stone" and the "tiny showers of gold." He feels himself "effusing and fluid, a phantom curiously floating, now here absorb'd and arrested" (514–15). While hinting that the scene is an allegory for the experience of aesthetic absorption or mystical concentration, the poem never completes the trope, but stays satisfied in merely suggesting it and reenacting for the reader the sensual experience of watching and hearing the grinder at work in the circle of children.

In "The Dalliance of the Eagles" of 1880, a poem that reports on seeing the big birds of prey mating on the wing, the title presents a contrast between the eagles' wild coupling and the daintier human interchange known as "dalliance." The human side of the story is suggested only in the title, however. In the poem proper, the reader sees only the observing speaker on his daily walk, gazing without comment on the sudden furor in the skies that ends with the male and female "parting, talons loosing, / Upward again on slow-firm pinions slanting, their separate diverse flight, / She hers, he his, pursuing" (412).

Some of the best examples of this kind of work appeared first in *Drum-Taps.* Having quickly burnt out his passion to rouse the masses to the Union's cause in the recruitment poems, Whitman discovered a way of communicating the solemnity and concentration of war – its way of confounding commentary and defying the facile moralizing of the preacher – in such poems as "Bivouac on a Mountainside." Here the dignity and power of the army at camp – "The numerous camp-fires scatter'd near and far, some away up on the mountain, / The shadowy forms of men and horses, looming, large-sized, flickering" – are communicated by the simple juxtaposition with and implied comparison to the sky full of the alternating light and shadow of flickering stars: "And over all the sky – the sky! far, far out of reach, studded, breaking out, the eternal stars" (435). The light touch of the sketch stops short of explicitly contrasting the ephemeral camp and vulnerability of the troops with the relative immortality of the stars "far out of reach." Whitman leaves the work of completing the impression to the eyes and sensibility of the reader.

Other *Drum-Taps* poems in this vein include "An Army Corps on the March" and "By the Bivouac's Fitful Flame." In these, Whitman joined a few other contemporaries (notably Herman Melville, another Civil War poet, who experimented with uninterpreted visual imagery in such poems as "The Maldive Shark") in anticipating the poetry of twentieth-century modernism. His poems in this vein foreshadowed the kind of observational lyric associated with the imagist movement led by Ezra Pound or the objectifying approach to poetic observation in the work of William Carlos Williams. In pieces like Pound's famous two-line poem "In a Station at the Metro" (in which "faces in the crowd" appear as "Petals on a wet, black bough"), the imagists followed Whitman in focusing the transformative poetic gaze upon single impressions. Likewise in poems like the notorious "The Red Wheelbarrow" ("so much depends / upon / a red wheel / barrow . . ."), Williams follows Whitman in pursuing the meaning of things-in-themselves without the interpretive apparatus and moralizing trends of traditional poetry.[6]

Perhaps the best example of the imagist trend in *Drum-Taps* is "Cavalry Crossing a Ford," in which Whitman traces the movements of troops across a river: "A line in long array where they wind betwixt green islands, / They take a serpentine course, their arms flash in the sun – hark to the musical clank" (435). Much like Pound's "In a Station at the Metro," Whitman's poem resists the urge to sermonize but nevertheless uses the devices of poetic association (metaphor and metonymy in this case) to hint at tension between the human and natural world. The cavalry crossing the water resembles a river itself. It takes a "serpentine course," and like the "silvery river," the soldiers' armaments "flash in the sun." But the "clank," which may sound "musical" to the poet's ear, also suggests the presence of industrial civilization and the sad work of war. Even though the poet refrains from questioning the naturalness of a long line of men on horseback, fully armed and organized into flagged units (called "columns" in military terminology, a rational arrangement like the "columns and graphs" of the lecturing astronomer), the contrast to the river suggests the failure of humankind to integrate smoothly with the natural environment.[7]

The emergence of the image poem in *Drum-Taps* reveals the poet's increasing preoccupation with the literate world and the printed text. Whitman began to make his reading a more prominent part of his writing. "Cavalry Crossing a Ford," for example, is not based on direct observation but is rather a poetic framing and light revision of a news story he read during the war. Whitman continued to draw upon his reading of the news for imagery as his deteriorating health limited his time outdoors. He discovered imagery to convey his experience of old age, for example, in a story about the Arctic explorer Greely who was cheered in the desolate landscape when he heard "the song of a single snow-bird merrily sounding over the desolation." It was not the song, however, so much as the account of the song in print and the scene of the Arctic landscape that most fully captured the poet's imagination, providing visual imagery for the persistent chill of "Old age land-lock'd within its winter bay . . . / These snowy hairs, my feeble arm, my frozen feet, / . . . sluggish floes, pack'd in the northern ice, the cumulus of years" (623).

One group of late-life poems that was based on direct observations of nature was "Fancies at Navesink," composed during a boating trip with his friend, the naturalist John Burroughs. The series, published as part of the "Sands at Seventy" annex to *Leaves of Grass*, documents Whitman's struggle with the limits of the visual experience and human understanding in an extended meditation on the mystery of the wave, the same ebb and flow which inspired the imagery of many earlier poems, but whose fullness continued to elude him. In the Navesink poems, he says he would "gladly barter" the powers of a Homer or Shakespeare if the sea would teach him the elusive lesson of natural poetry: "Would you the undulation of one wave, its trick to me transfer" (618). The tide that Whitman had boldly figured as the tongue of the sea lapping his bare feet in "Out of the Cradle" now resists his poetic striving. He confesses in another Navesink poem that the contemplation of waves only throws him back upon himself: "In every crest some undulating light or shade – some retrospect, / . . . Myself through every by-gone phase – my idle youth – old age at hand" (619–20).

In becoming the poet of the resisting image, Whitman completes his late-career transformation from the poet-prophet who makes the printed page sing and preach to the modern writer who muses over eye-appealing but often puzzling pictures. "Could but thy flagstones, curbs, façades, tell their inimitable tales," he writes in the poem "Broadway," but the pavement tells no tales; the poet confronts an unyielding image: "Thou, like the parti-colored world itself – like infinite, teeming, mocking life! / Thou visor'd, vast, unspeakable show and lesson" (624). This image of the poet alternately contented and frustrated with offering the uninterpreted picture contrasts strongly with the poet of the 1855 poem "Faces," who confidently attaches an interpretation to each impression that greets him on the street. No face can hide its inner condition from the poet as seer (or phrenologist): "Faces of friendship, precision, caution, suavity, ideality, / The spiritual prescient face, the always welcome common benevolent face" (125), "these faces bear testimony slumbering or awake" (127). The tendency of things to hold back their secrets was an idea that Whitman explored in his treatment of nature as early as 1856, in the poems that would become "This

Compost" and "Song of the Rolling Earth," but by "Sands at Seventy" the trend has extended to built environments and, to some extent, people. In "Broadway," the poet can only wonder "what passions, winnings, losses, ardors, swim thy waters" and guess at the "curious questioning glances" that, once signs of clear messages, now appear as "glints of love! / Leer, envy, scorn, contempt, hope, aspiration!" (624). Hinting at uncertainty and indirection, the word "glints" points toward one of Whitman's most famous remarks on poetics, from the 1867 poem "When I Read the Book": "Why even I myself I often think know little or nothing of my real life, / Only a few hints, a few diffused faint clews and indirections" (171).

"Faint clews and indirections" is a poetic summation often applied to Whitman's poetic method, but it does not seem particularly appropriate to the aggressively self-assured poems of 1855, to "Song of Myself," "The Sleepers," and "Faces." It fits best with the more circumspect and agnostic skepticism that sharply distinguishes Whitman's most modernist moods from the Romantic-Transcendental approach to the world that he inherited from Wordsworth and Emerson and put to work in the earlier poems.

Minor poetic modes

Occasional poems

In the first edition of *Leaves of Grass*, two of the twelve untitled poems were motivated by specific occasions and offer a kind of editorial response to these specific historical events. "Europe, the 72d and 73d Years of These States" responds to the European revolutions of 1848, and "A Boston Ballad" refers to an incident involving the return of a fugitive slave to his master. These previously published poems were the product of Whitman's earlier work in literary journalism and were possibly included to fill out the book when Whitman ran a little short on copy after including all the new poems composed specifically for the 1855 volume. While differing in style from the other poems, they certainly fit the book thematically and were kept in every edition thereafter.

One point that has been somewhat obscured by the tendency of scholars to see a narrative of development in Whitman's work – specifically a story of the young journalist transformed into an inspired poet in early middle age – is that Whitman never really stopped being a journalist. Even after he published *Leaves of Grass*, left the profession, and devoted himself to poetry, he steadily contributed opinion pieces, feature writing, public letters, and poems to newspapers and magazines in New York, Washington, and Philadelphia.

The work increased during the Civil War when Whitman's poetry and prose formed a kind of dialogue with the news, producing such noteworthy poems as "Cavalry Crossing a Ford" and the Lincoln elegies as well as the short prose sketches he would later collect in *Memoranda During the War*. Such writings suggest Whitman's desire to stay involved with the public life of his nation. After the war, this motive took on a special intensity as Whitman grew increasingly worried that people would forget the war and all it represented for the American people. He must have reasoned that if the war with which he came to identify his poetic mission were forgotten, he and his poetry could also fall into neglect. So to save what reputation he did have, he used his growing notoriety and name recognition, as well as his old connections in the press, to keep his name and his writing before the public on a regular basis.

After the war, an increasing percentage of the poetry that Whitman added to *Leaves of Grass* was first published in the periodical press, and many of the poems alluded or responded directly to topics and events of the day. The "Autumn Rivulets" cluster, added to *Leaves of Grass* in 1881 but drawing poems from many earlier editions, offers a particularly rich mix of occasional poems originally published in newspapers and magazines. The Civil War poem "The Return of the Heroes" was first published in *The Galaxy* in 1867. "The Singer in the Prison," which commemorates a concert in New York's Sing-Sing Prison, first appeared in Washington's *Saturday Evening Visitor* in 1869. "Warble for Lilac Time," one of Whitman's finest short lyrics in the Romantic vein, first celebrated the return of spring in *The Galaxy* in 1870. The occasional mode combined with the elegiac in Whitman's eulogy of the philanthropist George Peabody in "Outlines for a Tomb," first published in *The Galaxy* in 1870. And "An Old Man's Thought of School," celebrating the opening of a public school in Camden and dealing with education, a topic he frequently addressed in his early journalism, appeared first in the New York *Daily Graphic* in 1874. The trend continued in later clusters, reaching its zenith in the "First Annex: Sands at Seventy," appended to *Leaves of Grass* in 1888. This cluster was composed almost entirely of poems written under an open contract for the *New York Herald*.[8] It includes occasional pieces on such topics as the death of General Grant, the reburial of the Iroquois orator Red Jacket, and the completion of the Washington Monument.

As this brief overview suggests, the tone of the late occasional poems tends to be celebratory or commemorative, a trend that sometimes leads the poet in some surprising directions. The elegy for the millionaire Peabody, for example, commemorates a "lavish giver" (507) and supporter of the poor and the working class – actions and motives certainly meritorious but somewhat at odds with Whitman's usual insistence on the people's independence and self-sufficiency. "From Far Dakota's Cañons," first published in the New York

Tribune in 1876 and then included in the cluster "From Noon to Starry Night" in *Leaves*, offers a "trumpet-note for heroes" in response to the news of "Custer's Last Stand," the famous defeat of the flamboyant Civil War veteran and his troops at the hands of the Sioux people. Recent critics have, with some justice, though without acknowledging the historical context of broad public opinion, questioned Whitman's judgment in taking the vain and ambitious Custer, the very embodiment of the cruelest side of the genocidal policy of manifest destiny, as an exemplar of the "sternest heroism" in the "dark days" of Reconstruction after the war (592–3).

One of Whitman's most celebrated postwar poems, "Passage to India," is arguably an occasional poem that also accommodates manifest destiny, though not without some qualms. It was first published in 1871 in a booklet of its own with a few other poems, some previously published (including "A Noiseless, Patient Spider," with which it shares a tendency toward Transcendentalist abstraction and an encouragement of spiritual adventure). It was also included as a supplement to the 1871 *Leaves of Grass* and finally incorporated more smoothly into the whole. The composition of the poem dates from the late sixties and celebrates three technological achievements of that era: the completion of the transatlantic telegraph cable, the Suez Canal, and the Union and Central transcontinental railroad. Whitman obviously hoped to make extra money by publishing the work separately from *Leaves* and clearly saw the poem, like the Custer commemoration, as a way of finding something good to celebrate in the baleful context of Reconstruction. The poem acknowledges the positive accomplishments of modern humanity and the hope of creating connections among the different races of humankind, fulfilling the old dream of a passage to India that would eliminate the barriers to economic and cultural trade. The suggestion of a divine plan – "God's purpose from the first" (532) – hints strongly toward the doctrine of manifest destiny, according to which western civilization, goaded by American initiative and the pioneering spirit, would inevitably attain global ascendancy. After the western lands of the US were tamed and controlled, technological progress and development would continue to spread until the farthest reaches of the Far East were brought into the great circle.

Whitman may have inadvertently caught the spirit of the imperialist rhetoric that many politicians of the postwar years used to salve the wounded spirit of Euro-Americans whose homes and families had been damaged by the war. But, while the poem emulates the imperialist rhetoric, it is important to note that it dates from the same period as the prose work *Democratic Vistas* (discussed in Chapter 5), and like that work, it undercuts the celebration of technological modernism with an insistence that progress is worth nothing unless there is a spiritual dimension to every material gain. The poet's voice rises to challenge the exponents of material progress to discover the "Passage to more than India" (539). Only the discovery of cosmic unities will finally satisfy the inner drive of humanity to explore and claim new lands. Moreover, it is the poet and not the engineer or the conqueror who can show the way to God, the ultimate object of the human quest: "After the seas are all cross'd, (as they seem already cross'd,) / After the great captains and engineers have accomplish'd their work, / . . . The true son of God shall come singing his songs" (534).

While attempting to recover the transcendent vision and grand tone of the earlier cosmic dramas, however, "Passage to India" falls back upon standard poetic diction (such as "thee," "thou," and "pleasest") rather than relying on the vernacular inventiveness of the "language experiment" that had made *Leaves* a memorable and distinctive book. The sprawling and specific catalogues of images and vignettes of the earlier cosmic dramas are also missing from "Passage to India" as the poem drifts toward the abstraction of the world map and religious universalism. The expansive tropes of "Song of Myself" and "Crossing Brooklyn Ferry" give way to the master trope of exploration so that, while insisting on the priority of the poet-prophet, the language of the poet here actually depends upon the accomplishments of those he claims to outdo – the "great captains and engineers." In short, "Passage to India" is one of the best illustrations of how Whitman had lost his visionary impetus in the years after the war when his own health and the health of the nation, as he saw it, was broken. The poem's promotional rhetoric fails to hide his basic disappointment and growing discontent with the American experiment.

While the imagist poems of *Drum-Taps* and the later editions of *Leaves*, from "Cavalry Crossing a Ford" to "The Dalliance of the Eagles," show Whitman making inventive use of his journalistic tendencies – the influence of the print culture over the oral culture and the consequent transformation of vocalism into imagism – the most ambitious of the occasional poems, such as "Passage to India" and later "Song of the Exposition," show Whitman struggling to use his journalistic sensibilities to recover his self-image as poet-prophet and prop up his sagging optimism by appealing to the exploratory energies of the postwar period. The imagist experiment demonstrates the durability of his poetic genius, but the failure of the occasional poems to revive the old cosmic visions suggests his inability to sustain the prewar visionary impulse as well as the tension between the competing impulses to defy the materialism of the age and to accommodate it in his poetry.

Messenger poems

Whitman's insistent practice of addressing the reader as if in direct conversation ("I" to "you") and his frequent use of apostrophe (the trope of directly addressing an absent person or even an inanimate object – the earth, the ocean, the mockingbird, the very pavement of the city street) conspire to create a genre of short poems in *Leaves of Grass*. In the 1860 *Leaves*, a few of these works were clustered together under the title "Messenger Leaves," but were later distributed throughout the book.

With poems in this "messenger" mode, Whitman clearly falls into the English Romantic lineage. In such works as Shelley's "Ode to the West Wind" and "To a Skylark," Romanticism had extended the old tradition of verse letters and epistolary odes by applying the grand style of the ode in apostrophes to nature, thus suggesting the continued need for, or recovery of, intimacy with nature in an era of urban expansion and industrialization. In America, the tradition prevailed in such popular poems as "To a Waterfowl" by William Cullen Bryant, the New York journalist and poet whom Whitman admired as a young man. Whitman took the tradition to new lengths, substituting his free verse for the highly stylized verse forms of the ode, and expanding the intimacy of the genre to include the likes of prostitutes, felons, strangers, technological objects ("To a Locomotive in Winter"), and even the reader.

Whitman was fond of using apostrophe in his longer poems in every mode, but as he grew more inclined to publish short works, the messenger poems emerged as a fairly well-defined genre. Often addressed in their titles with the preposition "to," the messenger poems serve Whitman's interest in portraying himself as a common man and a natural creature on speaking terms with ordinary people as well as with the noble ("To a President," addressed indirectly to James Buchanan), the natural ("To the Sun-set Breeze"), and the divine ("To Him That Was Crucified"). In "To a Common Prostitute," one of the original 1860 "Messenger Leaves," the Whitman persona is at once the natural man ("Walt Whitman, liberal and lusty as nature") and a seeming avatar of the figure of Christ who forgave the woman taken in adultery. "I charge you that you make preparation to be worthy to meet me," he tells the prostitute, "And I charge you that you be patient and perfect till I come" (512). In "You Felons on Trial in Courts," he takes a slightly different approach, but with a similar attitude of democratic inclusiveness. "I walk with delinquents with passionate love," he claims. Having known "hell's tides" first-hand, he says, "I feel I am of them – I belong to those convicts and prostitutes myself" (511). The confessional and intimate tone extends in "Calamus" to the anonymous eyes that Whitman encounters on the streets of the city ("To a Stranger" and "To a Western Boy").

Whitman's habit of addressing the reader directly in the apostrophe comes into play in several of the messenger poems. Two different poems, dating from 1856 and 1860, were ultimately titled "To You." Both use the contact with the reader through the medium of the book held close for reading as a metaphor for a revised author–audience relation that defies the usual assumption of distance and cold formality. The old taboo against fraternizing with strangers is boldly challenged in these poems, as well as in the messenger poems in "Calamus" with their suggestion of an almost casual promiscuity. The theme comes to fruition in the masterful farewell poem of 1860, "So Long." "Camerado, this is no book," Whitman tells the reader, "Who touches this touches a man / . . . I spring from the pages into your arms – decease calls me forth" (611). The poetic relation of I and you thus becomes, for Whitman, fully erotic: "Your breath falls around me like dew, your pulse lulls the tympans of my ears, / I feel immerged from head to foot, / Delicious, enough" (611).

In his later years, Whitman went back to the Romantic roots of the messenger leaves with nature poems like "To the Man-of-War-Bird" of 1876 (probably influenced by the ornithologist Burroughs). One of the last poems he would ever write, and one of his most successful short lyrics, "To the Sun-set Breeze," draws strongly upon this tradition. In old age, the poet finds himself immobile and housebound in the summer heat, "sick, weak-down, melted-worn with sweat" (644), until he is graced by a refreshing wind that enters the windows and doors of his dwelling. He addresses the breeze as a muse, a spirit that revives for a moment the soul's creative power: "Thou, messenger-magical strange bringer to body and spirit of me / (Distances balk'd – occult medicines penetrating me from head to foot)" (645). The breeze awakens all the senses and inspires the poetic vision of distant places full of memory and meaning: "I feel the sky, the prairies vast – I feel the mighty northern lakes, / I feel the ocean and the forest – somehow I feel the globe itself swift-swimming in space" (645). He is "laved" by the breeze, and thus shows through this last intimacy of the messenger poems that he remains to the end the earth's own lover.

Prose works

Whitman published prose works his entire career. Among his best early writings was the series of newspaper essays called "The Sun-Down Papers" of 1838, and one of his final additions to *Leaves of Grass* was the prose essay included in "Good-Bye My Fancy," the second annex to the 1891 "Death-Bed Edition." If Whitman's half-century of prose writings survived without his poetry, however, we would remember him as a very minor writer, if at all. The fiction he wrote was confined to the period of his literary apprenticeship, and although some stories have caught the attention of modern biographers and critics – notably "Wild Frank's Return," "Death in the School-Room (a Fact)," and the temperance novel *Franklin Evans*, all written in the 1840s, when Whitman seems seriously to have considered a profession as a fiction writer – they are distinguished less for their artistic merit than for the insight they provide into the poet's life and his relation to the literary-historical context.

The same might be said for Whitman's nonfiction prose of the period before the publication of the first edition of *Leaves of Grass* in 1855. The book reviews give insights into Whitman's reading, some of the editorial journalism contributes to the development of his political thinking, and the feature writing in newspapers and magazines anticipates the persona of "Song of Myself" and other poems – the public poet as "flaneur" or "caresser of life." Overall, though, the journalism of Whitman's early years, like the poetry and fiction of those years, is not particularly memorable or original. With the journalism also comes the problem of attribution. How much of a given paper did Whitman actually write when he served as a staff reporter or editor, and how many of the views were really his own as opposed to those he was obligated to present as a representative of the paper's political party or publishing interests?[1]

Whatever can be said for the quality or originality of these early writings, it is clear that the creative impetus for fiction writing was totally absorbed by the production of poetry after 1855 and that Whitman's vocation as poet likewise overwhelmed his career aspirations as a newspaper reporter and editor. Yet the prose nonfiction continued to develop throughout Whitman's life, and though it nowhere attains the distinction in style and thinking that makes him a great poet, it does include some remarkable work that stands on its own. In particular, the Preface to the 1855 *Leaves of Grass*, the long 1871 essay *Democratic Vistas*, and the 1882 memoir *Specimen Days* have prompted the serious engagement of scholars and critics.

These major prose works often verge subtly toward the poetic even as they build upon Whitman's extensive experience as a journalist. As he came to see himself as a bardic poet in the 1850s, he tested the generic boundaries of poetry and prose, often obscuring the lines of demarcation completely. This trend is especially true in the 1855 Preface, which has the character of a poetic and political manifesto. Like the cosmic/dramatic poems, it ranges between oracular observations about the human character and sweeping catalogues of concrete images. Like the "messenger" poems, it experiments with addressing the reader directly – "I" to "you" – with a spiritual or political challenge. Its main contribution appears in statements of Whitman's views on poetics; nowhere does he delineate the properties of great poetry and the great poet more directly and with greater passion and eloquence.

After the war, when Whitman had solidified his poetic self-concept to some degree, his stand-alone prose writings take on the character of the poet taking a prose vacation, trying on the looser fit of the prose paragraph but still drawing upon the styles, genres, and poetic modes that had made him famous on the literary scene. As with his best poems, he intermingles various modes to create shifting effects. *Democratic Vistas* mixes a cosmic and largely celebratory vision of democracy's future with a critical form of prophetic utterance not often seen in *Leaves of Grass*. It forcefully condemns the corruption and materialism that was threatening to wipe out the sacrifices of the Civil War by neglecting the spiritual and cultural promise of democracy and the Union. Though with less vituperation, *Democratic Vistas* displays the kind of tone and subject-matter previously engaged only in the unpublished pamphlet "The Eighteenth Presidency!" *Specimen Days*, which incorporates the earlier published *Memoranda During the War*, juxtaposes dark scenes of wartime life with bright sketches of nature and prose snapshots of travels that Whitman made in his later years, finishing with memorials to prominent literary figures of the age, moving from elegiac to imagistic and back again. *Democratic Vistas* thus expands upon the poet's prophetic repertoire, while *Specimen Days* experiments with new genres of prose, resonating with the current interest in "creative nonfiction," a category that includes not only memoir but also nature writing and travel literature.

The other prose works that Whitman published in the last two decades of his life tend to be retrospective and explanatory, a reexamination of his poetic motives and inspirations. At times, the poet appears most interested in justifying his mission in *Leaves of Grass*, interpreting his own work in light of literary history and the politics of the marketplace, or adding touches to his public persona. At other times, he feels the need to step out of his poetic persona and supplement his views on literary theory, nineteenth-century history, and democratic politics. In addition to providing insights into Whitman's biography and literary motives, the minor prose works are important mainly for the ways they reflect upon and supplement the poetry and advance the theory and practice of the "language experiment" to which Whitman devoted his life. But the late prose grows quickly repetitive as Whitman sounds his favorite themes – above all, those involving the prospects for democracy and a distinctive New World literature – and are often awkwardly stitched together or merely republished from shorter articles.

The three major works – the 1855 Preface, *Democratic Vistas*, and *Specimen Days* – if they do not exhaust the various themes and styles of Whitman's prose work, at least represent different periods of his mature writing (prewar, immediate postwar, and old age) and show the best examples of how Whitman uses different genres and methods of composition in sustained works of prose. These three works, therefore, take center stage in this chapter.

The 1855 Preface

The Preface to the 1855 *Leaves of Grass* is the most radically democratic, the most stylistically innovative, and the most Transcendental of Whitman's prose writings. A political and poetic manifesto, it stands with the first version of "Song of Myself" as the poet's Declaration of Independence for American poetry. Ironically, it may be the work in which Whitman is most dependent, in content and form, upon the influence of his predecessor, Ralph Waldo Emerson, the father of Transcendentalism, who also blurred the lines between oratorical and written performance and between prose and poetry.

As a work of patriotism and radical democracy, the Preface anticipates the poetry of 1855 in celebrating the appeal of the American character and landscape – "the roughs and beards and space and ruggedness and nonchalance that the soul loves" – and the abundance of the North American continent with its "crampless and flowing breadth" and its "prolific . . . extravagance" (5). He insists that "the genius of the United States is not best or most in its executives or legislatures, nor in its ambassadors or authors or colleges or churches or parlors, nor even in its newspapers or inventors . . . but always most in the common people" (5–6).

If the common people are themselves "unrhymed poetry," the emerging poet proclaims, they deserve a "gigantic and generous treatment" in literature (6). "The rhyme and uniformity of perfect poems," he says, "show the free growth of metrical laws and bud from them as unerringly and loosely as lilacs or roses on a bush, and take shapes as compact as the shapes of chestnuts and oranges and melons and pears, and shed the perfume impalpable to form" (11). In this organic theory of poetry, in which the form mirrors the values of the content, conforming not to convention but to the immediate needs of theme and emotion, Whitman provides a motive for the unrhymed and "crampless" verse that follows the Preface.

As if unable to contain the language experiment, however, the Preface itself begins to enact the principles it sets forth. The thematic organization of the whole, which proceeds almost by free association, and the paratactic structure of the prose – loose sentences and phrases strung together with "and" – suggest at once the overflowing abundance of the American land and the speech of the orator carried away with himself. The mention of a river or a tree quickly expands into a catalogue – "Mississippi with annual freshets and changing chutes, Missouri and Columbia and Ohio and Saint Lawrence with the falls and beautiful masculine Hudson," "the growths of pine and cedar and hemlock and liveoak and locust and chestnut and cypress" – and the list goes on (7). Just as lines overflow their endings in the verse form of the poems, the available punctuation seems unable to contain the extravagance of the prose in the Preface. The most obvious example is the use of multiple periods. The three periods conventionally used as an ellipsis in modern English appear to indicate something more here, expanding and contracting in number, from two to nine, perhaps to indicate the length of pauses or breaths between bursts of prose. The same technique appears in the 1855 poems, but disappears in later editions, following the tendency to move from an attempt to represent an oral culture on the printed page to a more conventional print literacy (see Chapter 4).

The constraints of genre likewise give way in the 1855 Preface. In the middle of his exposition of poetic principles, for example, Whitman launches into a how-to passage that prepares aspiring poets for success. Addressing the reader directly, he more or less gives the formula to which he attributes his own success – both as poet and person:

Love the earth and sun and the animals, despise riches, give alms to every one that asks, stand up for the stupid and crazy, devote your income and labor to others, hate tyrants, argue not concerning God, have patience and indulgence toward the people, take off your hat to nothing known or unknown or to any man or number of men, go freely with powerful uneducated persons and with the young and with the mothers of families. (11)

To these instructions, which make little or no distinction between good poetry and good living, he adds a syllabus for good reading, beginning (as one would expect from the author of "Song of Myself") with his own book: "read these leaves in the open air every season of every year of your life, re-examine all you have been told at school or church or in any book, dismiss whatever insults your own soul" (11). The result of such habits of action, reading, and thought is living poetry: "your very flesh shall be a great poem and have the richest fluency not only in its words but in the silent lines of its lips and face and between the lashes of your eyes and in every motion and joint of your body" (11).

As this passage suggests, the body proves as central a concern in the Preface as it does in the poetry. Again the strong materialist strain is tempered by a Transcendentalist insistence on the spiritual responsibilities of the great poet. If anything, the emphasis on the soul is stronger in the Preface than in the poems. "The land and sea, the animals fishes and birds, the sky of heaven and the orbs, the forests mountains and rivers, are not small themes," Whitman writes, but adds, "folks expect of the poet to indicate more than the beauty and dignity which always attach to dumb real objects . . . they expect him to indicate the path between reality and their souls" (10). Though he proclaims "the love between the poet and the man of demonstrable science," he also insists, "Exact science and its practical movements are no checks on the greatest poet but always his encouragement and support" (15). The poet is held up as the great exemplar of soulfulness and oneness with nature: "The known universe has one complete lover and that is the greatest poet" (11). But like Emerson, who in his "Divinity School Address" chastised Christians for missing the key message of the Gospels that Jesus came to declare not only his own oneness with God but that of all people, Whitman insists that poets have no special claim on soulfulness except the responsibility to connect others with their own souls. "The messages of great poets to each man and woman," he writes, "are Come to us on equal terms, Only then can you understand us, We are no better than you, What we enclose you enclose, What we enjoy you may enjoy" (14). Also like Emerson, Whitman favors personal spirituality over formal religion and priestcraft. "There will soon be no more priests," he writes, "A superior breed shall take their place . . . the gangs of kosmos and prophets en masse shall take their place. A new order shall arise and they shall be the priests of man, and every man shall be his own priest" (24–5). Whitman shares with Emerson and other prophetic writers of the time (including Abraham Lincoln in his near-future presidential addresses) a tendency to poeticize prose and employ a biblical style on the way to replacing the priest with the poet and ordinary seeker of spiritual truth. Another key aspect of Emerson's style – his sententiousness, or use of the "quotable quote" – appears prominently in the Preface (as nowhere else in Whitman's prose works). "All beauty comes from beautiful blood and a beautiful brain," Whitman writes, for example (11); or "In the beauty of poems are the tuft and final applause of science" (15).

The obviousness of Emerson's influence may account for Whitman's later inclination to abandon the original version of the Preface.[2] He distributed pieces of it in various poems, most generously in "By Blue Ontario's Shore." When it was republished in the 1882 collection of prose, *Specimen Days and Collect,* Whitman conventionalized the punctuation and cut the copy by one third. Apart from the obvious influence of Emerson, especially his essay "The Poet," which Whitman had heard as a lecture in 1842, the Preface may have come to seem to him a product of his overenthusiastic, almost manic entrance into modern poetry. By the 1880s, when he regularized and abbreviated the Preface, he was trying to minimize the influence of Emerson – omitting him entirely from a list of influences in "A Backward Glance O'er Travel'd Roads," published with *November Boughs* in 1888 – and his prose had grown more conventional as he came to question his own most avant-garde decisions. In the preface to *November Boughs,* he attributed the failure of the public to respond to his poetry partly to his radical experiments in form. The public response itself may account for his increasing embarrassment over the 1855 Preface, which ended with the bold and all-too-quotable sentence, "The proof of a poet is that his country absorbs him as affectionately as he has absorbed it" (26).

Democratic Vistas

Democratic Vistas, which appeared as an eighty-four-page pamphlet in 1871, was patched together from three essays composed in the late 1860s (two of which were published in the periodical press) in response to Thomas Carlyle's attack on democracy in *Shooting Niagra: And After?* While Whitman follows Carlyle and a number of other late-century writers (primarily English) in admitting that democracy had not produced a great literature, moral character, and culture to match its material achievements, he insists that, once it has run its course, democracy will be justified as the highest form of government.

The prose works written on the heels of the 1855 *Leaves*, such as the unpublished *Eighteenth Presidency!* and the public "Letter to Ralph Waldo Emerson" published with the 1856 *Leaves of Grass*, resemble the 1855 Preface in using a style that incorporates many of the features of Whitman's poetry. But *Democratic Vistas* features a style that Whitman would use frequently in his late prose, involving long periodic sentences with multiple qualifiers and complex syntax. While still employing some techniques of his poetic style, such as the occasional catalogue, generally the language of *Vistas* represents a departure from earlier writings. While the tone is prophetic, the style often suggests ambivalence and uncertainty, as if the poet was hesitant to state his views forthrightly or even unsure of his claims for democracy. He is most forthright in his critique of American society and literature, and most circuitous and uncertain-seeming in his projections of future success, with the result that the critique remains memorable while the positive force of the essay dissipates. Overall, the pace is sluggish, the organization loose and highly repetitive, and the points of his argument slow to emerge and ultimately too abstract and unclear about what the poet would have people do to realize the high promise of democracy in the New World. Even so, the essay merits attention as an extended example of Whitman's postwar thought on politics and poetics. It is also useful as a gauge of how deep his dissatisfaction with American culture had grown in the troubled period of Reconstruction.

The political argument begins with a thesis that he works out more positively in "Passage to India," a poem composed and published in the same years as *Vistas*. In the poem and the essay, Whitman contends that the material accomplishments of a society mean nothing without a corresponding spiritual development. But neither in "Passage to India" nor anywhere else in *Leaves of Grass* is Whitman as vehement in denouncing social backwardness and political corruption as he is in *Vistas*. While briefly hailing achievements in agriculture, industry, and technology with "pride and joy" (936), he follows with a much longer and more strongly worded lament for a society that has grown "canker'd, crude, superstitious, and rotten," in which "the moral conscience" is "either entirely lacking, or seriously enfeebled or ungrown" (937). He castigates the "depravity of the business classes," whose "sole object is, by any means, pecuniary gain," and denounces "fashionable life" for its "flippancy, tepid amours, weak infidelism, small aims, or no aims at all, only to kill time" (937). The conclusion is inescapable: "our New World democracy, however great a success in uplifting the masses out of their sloughs . . . is, so far, an almost complete failure in its social aspects, and in really grand religious, moral, literary, and esthetic results"; it is like a "vast and more and more thoroughly appointed body . . . with little or no soul" (938). And the body itself is not the healthy body he celebrates in his poems, but a degenerate, diseased, corrupted body: "everywhere the youth [is] puny, impudent, foppish, prematurely ripe – everywhere an abnormal libidinousness, unhealthy forms, male, female, painted, faded, dyed, chignon'd, muddy complexions, bad blood, the capacity for good motherhood deceasing or deceas'd, shallow notions of beauty, with a range of manners . . . probably the meanest to be seen in the world" (939).

In a footnote to this passage, he singles out women as particularly vulnerable or subject to a morally enfeebled material culture. The very capacity that makes women, in Whitman's view, superior to men – namely, "their powers of sane athletic maternity" – is most endangered. A "reconstructed sociology," he says, depends "on a new birth, elevation, expansion, invigoration of woman" (939–40n.). The point is so crucial (or his editing of the three original essays so faulty) that he repeats it later in the main text (in a sentence that nicely illustrates the straining style of *Vistas*):

> The idea of women of America, (extricated from this daze, this fossil and unhealthy air which hangs about the word *lady*,) develop'd, raised to become the robust equals, workers, and, it may be, even practical and political deciders with the men – greater than man, we may admit, through their divine maternity, always their towering, emblematical attribute – but great, at any rate, as man, in all departments; or, rather, capable of being so, soon as they realize it, and can bring themselves to give up toys and fictions, and launch forth, as men do, amid real, independent, stormy life. (955–6)

Later in the essay, as a corrective to this troubled state of female life, Whitman offers examples of independent womanhood – a seamstress, a business woman, and his own widowed mother – that provide a more concrete picture than the general portrait of ideal manhood he offers. But his prospect for women, built on these meager cases, remains somewhat more restricted than what he offers for men. Taken as a whole, the way he mixes radical egalitarianism and respect for the working woman into the basic sentimentality and condescension of his overall view sets Whitman apart from his contemporaries who would restrict women to exclusively domestic roles or have them conform to the "cult of true womanhood." But he shares with many writers in Victorian England and America a view of women as especially problematical in the full development of society and culture.

Like a number of the cosmic dramas among his poems, such as "The Sleepers," "This Compost," and "Passage to India" itself, *Democratic Vistas* eventually turns toward a hopeful affirmation after probing the depths, though here the movement is slower and seemingly less confident. When he does turn, it is the memory of the war and his faith in the individual, expressed as the key points of a personalist philosophy, that hold the greatest promise in Whitman's mind. He argues, for example, that any doubt about the personal integrity of the individuals that American democracy has produced should have been dispelled by the performance of soldiers on both sides of the Civil War. His first-hand experience bolsters this view: "Let no tongue ever speak in disparagement of the American races, north or south, to one who has been through the war in the great army hospitals" (946). His wartime experience provides the most vivid imagery in the essay, the rare break in its trend toward sweeping generalizations and philosophical abstraction: "We have seen [these soldiers] in trench, or crouching behind breastwork, or tramping in deep mud, or amid pouring rain or thick-falling snow, or under forced marches in hottest summer (as on the road to get to Gettysburg) – vast suffocating swarms, divisions, corps, with every single man so grimed and black with sweat and dust, his own mother would not have known him" (945). The witness of these soldiers – "the great bulk bearing steadily on, cheery enough, hollow-bellied from hunger, but sinewy with unconquerable resolution" (945) – keeps Whitman's faith in democracy alive.

This strong "common aggregate of living identities" will, according to the Hegelian outline that Whitman posits in the middle section of the essay, sustain the spirit of the whole during the course of a three-stage development, the "fruition" of which "resides altogether in the future" (956). Still in "its embryo condition" (959) democracy has passed successfully through two stages – first the establishment of a government and second the securing of "material prosperity" for the great majority of common people. The third stage, yet to be realized, is to foster a great democratic culture "to be evidenced by original authors and poets to come, by American personalities, plenty of them, male and female . . . and by native superber tableaux and growths of language, songs, operas, orations, lectures, architecture – and by a sublime and serious Religious Democracy" (977). "As fuel to flame, and flame to the heavens," Whitman writes, "so must wealth, science, materialism – even this democracy of which we make so much – unerringly feed the highest mind, the soul" (986).

Following the anti-clericalism that he inherited from his father's generation of free-thinkers and children of the French and American Revolutions – an ideology that he kept alive throughout his career – Whitman takes the responsibility for the soul's development away from the church and places it squarely in the hands of the poet: "The priest departs, the divine literatus comes" (932). Indeed Whitman's main intention in treating politics in *Democratic Vistas* is to provide a grounding for a discussion of poetics. "What I say in these Vistas," he says, "has its main bearing on imaginative literature, especially poetry, the stock of all" (934). Whitman could hardly think of poetics as separate from politics, so that the idea that a political economy could develop without a corresponding development in national poetry could only seem to him a serious problem of spiritual balance, even a perversion of human culture.

The literary theory he advances resumes some of the arguments from 1855, but also exhibits some differences. For one thing, the concept that the common people embody a form of living poetry has disappeared while the concept of secular poetry as a new priesthood remains. The life of the mind takes on a new grandeur in *Democratic Vistas*: "a single new thought, imagination, abstract principle, even literary style, fit for the time, put in shape by some great literatus, and projected among mankind, may duly cause changes, growths, removals, greater than the longest and bloodiest war, or the most stupendous merely political, dynastic, or commercial overturn" (933–4). While he had insisted on being the "poet of the body" as well as the poet of the soul in 1855, by 1871, the emphasis seems to have shifted in the other direction. Not only do the people need the poet to show them the connection between material life and the life of the soul, as he said in the 1855 Preface; now they need the poet to help them rise out of the slough of material life and realize a religious ideal. The shift is subtle, but significant – a slight diminishment of faith in the spiritual power of the people and a slight aggrandizement of the poet's role. The love of the people is still there, no doubt. "When I pass to and fro . . . beholding the crowds of the great cities," Whitman writes, "when I mix with these interminable swarms of alert, turbulent, good-natured, independent citizens, mechanics, clerks, young persons – at the idea of this mass of men, so fresh and free, so loving and so proud, a singular awe falls upon me" (954–5). Musing on these people, the poet observes "with dejection and amazement, that among our geniuses and talented writers or speakers, few or none have yet really spoken to this people, created a single image-making work for them, or absorb'd the central spirit and the idiosyncracies which are theirs" (955).

Of course, this critique begs the question: What about *Leaves of Grass*? Very likely, some of the tone of disappointment that pervades *Democratic Vistas* derives from the poet's sense that his own work had failed. The use of the word "absorb'd" in this context recalls the line from the 1855 Preface about the country's affectionate absorbing of the poet. By the time he wrote *Vistas*, Whitman certainly had his share of admirers – the Boston transcendentalists, the New York bohemians, the Washington circle that included William Douglas O'Connor and John Burroughs, and most recently, an enthusiastic English readership led by William Rossetti and the Pre-Raphaelites. But this audience at home and abroad was composed primarily of upper-middle-class intellectuals and fellow writers; he could hardly think that the common people of his country had "absorbed" him. So Whitman may have counted himself among the "few" who had captured the spirit of the people in his poetry, but more likely, at this point, he honestly doubted himself and concluded that he had not adequately passed the "proof of a poet." He may have worried that he had not been absorbed because he had failed to absorb the spirit of the people. The excitement of the orientation of the 1855 *Leaves* toward the present moment – the great Now of the spirit realized with the material intensity of bodily pleasure – had thus by 1871 yielded to the future orientation and more abstract spirituality of *Democratic Vistas*.

Specimen Days

By the time Whitman published *Specimen Days and Collect* in 1882, he appears to have recovered some of his equanimity and confidence. The difference between *Democratic Vistas* and *Specimen Days* is much like the difference between the late visionary poems such as "Passage to India" and "Song of the Redwood-Tree," in which the poet's lagging inspiration is bolstered by an imperious rhetoric of false confidence, and the more imagistic poems of *Drum-Taps* and the late editions of *Leaves of Grass*, in which the poet discovers new ways to realize the craft and joy of writing. While *Vistas* had been written in the period of ill health following his exhaustion in the Civil War and leading up to his paralytic stroke in 1873, Whitman wrote *Specimen Days* at a time when he was becoming adjusted to a more limited life as an old man with precarious health. As he entered his last decade of life, he was allowing himself to let go of the demanding role of poet-prophet of democracy and become the Good Gray Poet, reflecting on a long and eventful life and on the natural and social world that ever retained a fascination for him.

In the introduction to the 1882 volume, Whitman adopts a charming nonchalance in his approach, telling the reader that he merely "swooped" together the pieces of prose in the "Collect" section "like fish in a net" (690n). The "fish" included such trophies as *Democratic Vistas*, "A Memorandum at a Venture" (his most unified defense of his treatment of sexuality and the body in his poetry), the prefaces to *Leaves of Grass*, and a lecture on Lincoln. Even in the more purposeful *Specimen Days*, the aim of which he says is to satisfy the request of his friends to give some account of his life, he retains the quality of a "mélange" whose "lackings and wants of connection" must simply "take care of themselves" (689). Likely he overstates his lack of attention to what he considers "the most wayward, spontaneous, fragmentary book ever printed" (690) – especially as regards his claim to have published the notes he made during the Civil War and during his retreats to the country in later life more or less as he took them down at the time of the original composition. Such a claim can only raise doubts for anyone familiar with Whitman's inclination to tinker with his writings. But the book does indeed appear extremely loose and impressionistic – if not random, certainly an assorted collection of "specimens" of the poet's observations and thoughts. The tone of relaxed informality is reflected in the style, which differs strongly from the grand poetic style of the 1855 Preface and from the complex intensity of *Democratic Vistas*. Not quite conversational, the style is highly varied, as one would expect from a book pieced together from notebooks and previously published writings, but overall it retains a kind of comfortable simplicity and concreteness often lacking in his other prose works.

Specimen Days deserves the attention of students interested in the history of creative nonfiction. In this single volume, we find the leading poet of nineteenth-century America trying his hand at the three forms of nonfiction that since his time have become the primary genres of the popular essay: memoir, nature writing, and travel writing. The three genres more or less define a loose three-part structure in the book as a whole. The first section is fairly straightforward memoir with brief reminiscences of his early life and more extended sketches from the war years. The second section comprises the nature notes he wrote during visits to the country when he was living in Camden, New Jersey, in the early 1880s. In the writings of the third section, he ranges farther afield and produces something like a travel book, an account of trips west and north by train as well as of more metaphorical journeys involving places and people he has met through his reading and literary career. While retaining a disarming simplicity and directness – his heritage as a feature journalist perhaps – each segment of this rough three-part structure highlights different aspects of the poet-commentator on the scene as American history unfolds.

Memoir

Whitman starts with a few pages of straight autobiography, beginning with his genealogy and continuing with reflections on his youth and early manhood. He identifies "three sources and formative stamps to my own character." The first is the Dutch and English heritage of his mother and father, respectively, to which he attributes moral and psychological significance (such as the "subterranean tenacity and central bony structure" of "obstinacy, willfulness" he inherits from the English side of his father [705]). The second is the place where he grew up, Long Island, with its meadows and woods and wild seascapes contrasting with the rapidly developing urban centers of Brooklyn and, across the East River, Manhattan.[3] The third is the war, which clearly changed everything for Whitman.

He incorporates the bulk of his earlier published *Memoranda during the War* into *Specimen Days*, which until recently has offered the most accessible version of these remembrances. Both versions preserve some of the most moving and finely crafted prose that Whitman ever wrote, revealing him to have been a profoundly gifted war correspondent whose work anticipates famous journalist-authors of later years, such as Ambrose Bierce, Stephen Crane, and Ernest Hemingway.[4] The unity of the *Memoranda* volume as a treatment of the war may have been compromised to some degree by its inclusion in *Specimen Days*, but as a large component of Whitman's life and character, the war demanded treatment in his most extended autobiographical book. Whitman also wisely realized that the original publication of these fine prose sketches was too limited and would likely be overlooked.

As for the unity, it is not so much the unity of external events but that of Whitman's experience that makes *Specimen Days* work. In this sense, the incorporation of *Memoranda during the War* into the later volume is like the inclusion of *Drum-Taps* as a cluster in *Leaves of Grass*. Even before, when it was a stand-alone volume, *Drum-Taps* included some striking treatments of the nature/society rift, such as "Give Me the Splendid Silent Sun" and "When I Heard the Learn'd Astronomer." In such poems, Whitman lays a metaphysical foundation for a key theme that also proves significant in *Democratic Vistas* and *Specimen Days*, namely that democracy, like art, finds its bearings in dialectical interaction with nature (both human and nonhuman nature). The theme emerges explicitly in "Give Me the Splendid Silent Sun" and more subtly in imagistic poems like "Cavalry Crossing a Flood." It is treated most directly in the prose works. Recalling the theme of "This Compost" in *Democratic Vistas*, Whitman writes, "as, by virtue of its kosmical, antiseptic power, Nature's stomach is fully strong enough not only to digest the morbific matter always presented . . . , so [is] American democracy's" (949). Toward the end of *Specimen Days*, by way of conclusion, Whitman writes:

> Democracy most of all affiliates with the open air, is sunny and hardy and sane only with Nature – just as much as Art is. Something is required to temper both – to check them, restrain them from excess, morbidity . . . American Democracy, in its myriad personalities, in factories, work-shops, stores, offices – through the dense streets and houses of cities, and all their manifold sophisticated life – must either be fibred, vitalized, by regular contact with out-door light and air and growths, farm-scenes, animals, fields, trees, birds, sun-warmth and free skies, or it will certainly dwindle and pale. (925–6)

The nature–democracy dialectic, as much as the thread of experience from Whitman's own life, thus provides a unifying dimension in the otherwise loose weave of *Specimen Days*.

Specimen Days also shares with *Drum-Taps* the occasional use of narratives and scenes developed second-hand from newspaper reports, such as the account of the battle of Bull Run in *Specimen Days*. More importantly, the two works share a motivating exigence: the worry of the poet-journalist over the need to get history into words as it is happening. Under the headline "The Real War Will Never Get in the Books," Whitman picks two themes that are most likely to be lost. First, he is compelled to recount "the seething hell and the black infernal background of countless minor scenes and interiors" (778). He is less concerned with "the official surface-courteousness of the Generals" and "the few great battles," and more concerned with an honest account of the atrocities, the dying soldier's memories of the "surrender'd brother, and the mutilations of the corpse afterward," of the "carcasses . . . left for the citizens to bury or not, as they chose" (778–9). Second, he feels the need to preserve the "interior history" of the "actual soldier," his "incredible dauntlessness, habits, practices, tastes, language, his fierce friendship, his appetite, rankness, his superb strength and animality, lawless gait, and a hundred unnamed lights and shades of camp" (779). The atrocity of war and the character of the common soldier thus become the themes that most concern him in these prose memoirs (as well as in his poetry). Even if he knows he will inevitably fall short, as he suggests here, Whitman devotes himself to balancing the accounts of the official histories and polite accounts by bearing witness to the evils of war and the minutiae of human glory.

Both themes derive from his experience in the war hospitals. He records the stories of the atrocities that he has heard whispered from the very lips of the wounded and dying men he attended in the hospitals – *attended* in the double sense of caring for and listening to, the same attitude he hopes to inspire in the reader: pay attention! he seems to say, and don't cease to care about the sacrifice of the war. In a passage titled "A Glimpse of War's Hell-Scenes," he tells of an attack of mounted guerillas on a train of Union ambulances:

> No sooner had our men surrender'd, the rebels instantly commenced robbing the train and murdering their prisoners, even the wounded . . . Among the wounded officers in the ambulances were one, a lieutenant of regulars, and another of higher rank. These two were dragg'd out on the ground on their backs, and were now surrounded by the guerillas, a demoniac crowd, each member of which was stabbing them in different parts of their bodies. One of the officers had his feet pinn'd firmly to the ground by bayonets stuck through them and thrust into the ground.

These two officers, as afterwards found on examination, had receiv'd about twenty such thrusts, some of them through the mouth, face, &c. The wounded had all been dragg'd (to give a better chance also for plunder,) out of their wagons; some had been effectually dispatch'd, and their bodies were lying there lifeless and bloody. Others, not yet dead, but horribly mutilated, were moaning or groaning. Of our men who surrender'd, most had been thus maim'd or slaughter'd. (748)

In demonizing the enemy – the "demoniac crowd" of rebel rangers – Whitman follows a common rhetorical strategy of wartime propaganda. But he goes on to show how Union soldiers took their revenge with equal savagery. Demonization is not merely a rhetorical tactic for Whitman. It is an effect of war, which builds upon the predatory aspects of the human psyche. Moreover, he insists that the episode he narrates is not an isolated matter, but is all too typical:

> Multiply [the story] by scores, aye hundreds – verify it in all the forms that different circumstances, individuals, places, could afford – light it with every lurid passion, the wolf's, the lion's lapping thirst for blood – the passionate, boiling volcanoes of human revenge for comrades, brothers slain – with the light of burning farms, and heaps of smutting, smouldering black embers – and in the human heart everywhere black, worse embers – and you have an inkling of this war. (749)

The redeeming side of the story, in so far as there is redemption from such a terrifying reality, is the moral nature of the common soldier laid bare by hardship. Without sentimentalizing and always balancing his account of the men's superb character with the realism he summons in treating the atrocities not only of the battlefield but also of the hospital (never turning aside from the buckets of blood and stinking gangrene, the diarrhea and death), Whitman tells a moving tale of courage and loving comradeship in the scenes he witnesses in camp and hospital. He adds to the realism and immediacy of the text by including letters that he wrote to parents about their dead sons and dispatches he wrote to papers about news of the war. But the most moving passages are the simply written observations of life and death in the hospitals, which the poet renders with great care and attentiveness to nuance. "I have noticed through most of the hospitals," he writes in a segment headed "Death of a Wisconsin Officer," for example, "that as long as there is any chance for a man, no matter how bad he may be, the surgeon and the nurses work hard, sometimes with curious tenacity, for his life, doing everything, and keeping somebody by him to execute the doctor's orders, and minister to him every minute night and day. See that screen there. As you advance through the dusk of early candlelight, a nurse will step forth on tip-toe, and silently but imperiously forbid you to make any noise, or perhaps to come near at all. Some soldier's life is flickering there, suspended between recovery and death" (736). The imagery (the fine poetic touch of "flickering" to describe the soldier's life in the candlelit ward) and the shift of perspective from indicative to imperative to create a sense of immediacy in this passage nicely demonstrate the poetic strokes that Whitman would lightly apply in this prose experiment to preserve and protect the memories that he held sacred. He goes on here, as he does in numerous passages, to show the sense of community that he shared with the doctors, nurses, and soldiers in the horrible but somehow holy place, even as he advances his story of the coming of death:

> The neighboring patients must move in their stocking feet. I have several times been struck with such mark'd efforts – everything bent to save a life from the very grip of the destroyer. But when that grip is fix'd, leaving no hope or chance at all, the surgeon abandons the patient. . . . [The] nurse gives him milk-punch or brandy, or whatever is wanted, *ad libitum*. There is no fuss made. Not a bit of sentimentalism or whining have I seen about a single death-bed in hospital or on the field, but generally impassive indifference. All is over, as far as any efforts can avail; it is useless to expand emotions or labors. While there is any prospect they strive hard . . .; but death certain and evident, they yield the field. (736)

The chief feature of Whitman's prose in such passages, a feature that distinguishes these specimens from his poetry and previous prose works, is a remarkable restraint in both tone and style. The restraint in the language complements fully the attitude of impassivity and solemnity in the face of wartime death, the resignation and acceptance of the inevitable he describes in this fine passage. Whitman maintains the restrained style not only in this passage but also when he reports on the rushed and sometimes confused activity of the hospitals and the perplexity that often greets visitors. Even his profound admiration for the men finds expression in relatively understated terms – short sentences, plain statements, fewer adjectives, more highly selected images, and more straightforwardly narrated actions – compared at least to the effusive bursts of the 1855 Preface and the elaborated style of *Democratic Vistas*. As he watches the columns of men on the field one day, he writes, for example, "Along and along they filed by me, with often a laugh, a song, a cheerful word, but never once a murmur. It may have been odd, but I never before so realized the majesty and reality of the American people en masse. It fell upon me like a great awe." Having made the observation, he proceeds right along with the narrative, like the column itself moving in the night: "The strong ranks moved neither fast nor slow," and so on (740). In this respect, *Specimen Days* partakes of the movement in Whitman's late poetry away from preaching and prophesy. He is more inclined to let the actions and images mostly speak for themselves, while he is content to fill his role as witness to history with occasional light commentary.

Nature writing

As in *Drum-Taps*, nature forms an important backdrop and contrast to the scene of war in *Specimen Days*. In the war memoirs, Whitman complements his treatments of the psychological subtleties of human nature that appear in atrocities and heroic comradeship (among doctors and nurses as well as soldiers) with sketches of brief and poetic encounters with the natural earth. In "A Silent Night Ramble," nature appears not only as a retreat but as a way of breaking free from the confines of the tragic hospital atmosphere. Society is small and tight, nature large and liberating. Its refreshing silence stands in contrast to the moans and screams of the sick ward and the clank and holler of battle: "To-night, after leaving the hospital at 10 o'clock, (I had been on self-imposed duty some five hours, pretty closely confined,) I wander'd a long time around Washington. The night was sweet, very clear, sufficiently cool, a voluptuous half-moon, silently golden, the space near it of a transparent blue-gray tinge" (738). In other memoranda, Whitman wonders about the way the weather seems at times to sympathize with the surges and calms of the war, providing meaningful signs and portents to the observant mind, such as the "western star, Venus" that would become a key symbol in "When Lilacs Last in the Dooryard Bloom'd." In those days, Whitman reports, Venus had never seemed so large and bright, "as if it held rapport indulgent with humanity, with us Americans" (760).[5] But nature more commonly forms a comforting contrast to the hubbub and struggles of human society. In the "Silent Night" sketch, Whitman feels tired after his work, but as for nature and even the quiet, empty edifice of the Patent Office at night, the human activity removed, "Somehow it look'd rebukefully strong, majestic there in the delicate moonlight" (738). Whitman closes the sketch with images that recall "When I Heard the Learn'd Astronomer," a poem first published in *Drum-Taps*: "The sky, the planets, the constellations all so bright, so calm, so expressively silent, so soothing, after those hospital scenes. I wander'd to and fro till the moist moon set, long after midnight" (738).

By juxtaposing memoirs of the war with his nature sketches of the early 1880s that he added to in *Specimen Days*, Whitman drives toward the conclusion of a chastened Romantic: war's damage can be healed only by a return to the ways of the earth, a retreat from the demands of society. The poet uses his own damaged old body to stand for the wounded body politic, much as his healthy body had represented the promise of democracy in "Song of Myself" and as the death of Lincoln had represented the sacrifice of the whole nation in "When Lilacs Last in the Dooryard Bloom'd." Indeed, the *Specimen* sketch entitled "A Sun-Bath – Nakedness" comes close to recovering the spirit of the 1855 "Song of Myself" – or at least an attractively mellow, old-age version of "the merge." "It seems as if peace and nutriment from heaven subtly filter into me as I slowly hobble down these country lanes and across fields, in the good air," he writes, "as I sit here in solitude with Nature – open, voiceless, mystic, far removed, yet palpable, eloquent Nature. I merge myself in the scene, the perfect day" (806). Like an army after battle, he says, "Here I retreated every hot day" and "seem'd to get identity with each and every thing around me, in its condition. Nature was naked, and I was also" (806–7). The "rapport" he hypothesized between weather and war in the earlier memoranda is realized in these sun baths by Timber Creek, leading the poet to muse that "the inner never lost rapport we hold with earth, light, air, trees, &c., is not realized through eyes and mind only, but through the whole corporeal body, which I will not have blinded or bandaged any more than the eyes. Sweet, sane, still Nakedness in Nature! – ah if poor, sick, prurient humanity in cities might really know you once more!" (807–8).

Nature in the second half of *Specimen Days* is largely represented in this way – from the dominant perspective of urban life – much as nature in the first half is set in contrast to war. The earth is something to come back to – to return to, retreat to, recreate, recover. "After you have exhausted what there is in business, politics, conviviality, love, and so on – have found that none of these finally satisfy, or permanently wear – what remains?" the poet asks. "Nature remains; to bring out from their torpid recesses, the affinities of a man or woman with the open air, the trees, the fields, the changes of the seasons – the sun by day and the stars of heaven by night" (780–1). Using his old habit of direct address – "let me pick thee out singly, reader dear, and talk in perfect freedom, negligently, confidentially" (782) – the poet moves out of his confinement in convention as well as his confinement in the city. He moves into "soothing, healthy, restoration – after three years of paralysis – after the long strain of the war, and its wounds and death" (781). Now the confinement involves his own physical paralysis and infirmity, which resonates symbolically with the general condition of urban life:

> Away then to loosen, to unstring the divine bow, so tense, so long. Away, from curtain, carpet, sofa, book – from "society" – from city house, street, and modern improvements and luxuries – away to the primitive winding . . . , wooded creek, with its untrimm'd bushes and turfy

banks – away from the ligatures, tight boots, buttons, and the whole cast-iron civilizee life – from entourage of artificial store, machine, studio, office, parlor – from tailordom and fashion's clothes – from any clothes, perhaps, for the nonce, the summer heats advancing, there in those watery, shaded solitudes. (782)

And yet the natural is not necessarily or absolutely opposed to city life, as we see in a celebration of urban experience entitled "Human and Heroic New York." The seeming dissonance between the sentiments of this celebration and the exaltation of the Timber Creek retreat is resolved in Whitman's use of natural metaphors as well as contrasts in the treatment of nature and society. The city is praised not for its wealth and civilization so much as for its mass of people, the aggregate of ordinary bodies, and the raw human energy that speaks to the old poet's soul, the very kind of experience he finds in his nakedness at Timber Creek. He mingles in the "great seething oceanic populations," reviving the original spirit of "Crossing Brooklyn Ferry" (822). The flood tide of people metaphorically unites with the ocean itself, "bubbling and whirling and moving like its own environment of waters"; the "mighty channels of men" become "current humanity" – in both senses of current, the flow of water and the present time (823–4). The current presses toward the ideal merge of democracy, medicine for the old man's soul:

> In old age, lame and sick, pondering for years on many a doubt and danger for this republic of ours – fully aware of all that can be said on the other side – I find in this visit to New York, and the daily contact and rapport with its myriad people, on the scale of the oceans and tides, the best, most effective medicine my soul has yet partaken – the grandest physical habitat and surroundings of land and water the globe affords – namely, Manhattan island and Brooklyn. (824)

Yet there remains one current of humanity that runs against the poet's generally approving view – "the full oceanic tide of New York's wealth and 'gentility,'" on which he comments in a section entitled "A Fine Afternoon, 4 to 6": "Private barouches, cabs and coupés, some fine horseflesh – lapdogs, footmen, fashions, foreigners, cockades on hats, crests on panels" (845). The poet is prepared to be impressed by the show, open to it, but the impression fails when he encounters the actual bodies of the rich, and he resorts to the language of sickness and degeneracy that he had employed in *Democratic Vistas*: "Through the windows of two or three of the richest carriages I saw faces almost corpse-like, so ashy and listless" (845). He concludes that "the whole affair exhibited less of sterling America, either in spirit or countenance, than I had counted on from such a select mass-spectacle." Instead, the scene "confirms a thought that haunts me . . . namely, that they are ill at ease, much too conscious, cased in too many cerements, and far from happy – that there is nothing in them which we who are poor and plain need at all envy, and that instead of the perennial smell of the grass and woods and shores, their typical redolence is of soaps and essences, very rare may be, but suggesting the barber shop – something that turns stale and musty in a few hours anyhow" (845–6).

The distance from nature, from outdoor life, thus served Whitman as a figure for representing the difference between common humanity and the moneyed classes. He returns to the theme in the final section of *Specimen Days* (previously quoted) and uses it to bolster his theory of art and democracy as stemming from nature rather than from wealth and power.

Travel writing

The travel writing section of *Specimen Days* offers a prose variation on the imagist lyrics, the reportorial poems of *Drum-Taps* and late-life poems like "The Dalliance of the Eagles." A scene is represented with a minimum of commentary and the primary appeal is to the sense of sight. The prose treatment, however, takes on an element of tourism not obviously present in the poems. In "Seeing Niagara to Advantage," for example, Whitman reports on watching the famous falls from the platform of a slow-moving train:

> The river tumbling green and white, far below me; the dark high banks, the plentiful umbrage, many bronze cedars, in shadow; and tempering and arching all the immense materiality, a clear sky overhead, with a few white clouds, limpid, spiritual, silent. Brief, and as quiet as brief, that picture – a remembrance always afterwards. Such are the things, indeed, I lay away with my life's rare and blessed bits of hours, reminiscent, past. (877)

The Falls are silent, seen at a distance, framed photographically by technology – the experience of train travel. Gone now are the tactile impressions that mean so much in the early poems, along with the tastes and smells both pleasant and offensive from the nature poetry and war writings. Whitman seems to forget his own insistent advice that "rapport" with nature depends upon the "whole corporeal body" (807). The perspective and silence may be sublime, but nature is not fully responsible for the silence and the spectacle; it is technologically mediated, determined by the conditions of travel by rail.

The sense of sight predominates, filtered by technology and combined with the work of light and air. The scenic, photographic quality, a sort of poetic collecting of snapshots, becomes the norm in Whitman's travel notes.[6] The bard of democracy has become a tourist, though to his credit, he refuses to accept the standard agenda offered by the tourism industry emerging at the time alongside the technologies of rail travel and photography. In a specimen he calls "America's Characteristic Landscape," he celebrates the Great Plains – a sight notoriously difficult to photograph and slow to cross even by train. Yet he ranks the Plains higher than other vaunted sights in the tourist's repertoire. "I know the standard claim is that Yosemite, Niagara falls, the upper Yellowstone and the like, afford the greatest natural shows," he says, but he prefers the "Prairies and Plains," which "while less stunning at first sight, last longer, fill the esthetic sense fuller, precede all the rest, and make North America's characteristic landscape" (864). Far from empty, the Plains inspire a kind of prose poetry in Whitman, unfolding into a virtual portfolio or slide show of photographic images:

> My days and nights, as I travel here – what an exhilaration! – not the air alone, and the sense of vastness, but every local sight and feature. Everywhere something characteristic – the cactuses, pinks, buffalo grass, wild sage – the receding perspective, and the far circle-line of the horizon all times of day, especially forenoon – the clear, pure, cool, rarefied nutriment for the lungs, previously quite unknown – the black patches and streaks left by surface-conflagrations – the deep-plough'd furrow of the "fire-guard" – the slanting snow-racks built all along to shield the railroad from winter drifts – the prairie-dogs and the herds of antelope – the curious "dry rivers" – occasionally a "dug-out" or corral – Fort Riley and Fort Wallace – those towns of the northern plains, (like ships on the sea,) Eagle-Tail, Coyote, Cheyenne, Agate, Monotony, Kit Carson – with ever the ant-hill and the buffalo-wallow – ever the herds of cattle and the cow-boys ("cow-punchers") to me a strangely interesting class, bright-eyed as hawks, with their swarthy complexions and their broad-brimm'd hats – apparently always on horseback, with loose arms slightly raised and swinging as they ride. (863)

Scattered among the travel sketches are a few pieces of elegiac writing – memories of the fiery Quaker preacher Elias Hicks and the fellow poet and literary journalist Edgar Allan Poe, who lived and worked in New York during Whitman's literary apprenticeship, for example – and reflections prompted by the death of other major writers, such as Carlyle and Longfellow. On first reading, like the mix of war and nature writings, these eulogies seem to fit poorly with the travel essays. But they are gathered under the broader theme of life's journey, which in *Specimen Days* as in Emily Dickinson's poem "There Is No Frigate Like a Book," must include the imaginative journey of reading. Where Whitman's life journey intersected with that of other writers thus proves an appropriate topic in a large view of travel writing as autobiography.

Like *Leaves of Grass* in its final versions, *Specimen Days* comprises an account of a life seen from various perspectives and under the influence of varying methods and ideologies. It is loose and eclectic. The prose snapshots of the late-life travel sketches take their place with the poet-journalist's memoranda of the war and the poet-naturalist's specimens of life seen in its natural setting. Together, these different methods inform the best of Whitman's efforts to sustain an extended and original prose performance.

Chapter 6

Critical reception

In the 150 years since the first publication of *Leaves of Grass*, despite his late-life worries over the financial failure of his work and his then uncertain status in the hearts and minds of his fellow citizens, Whitman has certainly been absorbed into the canon of American and world literature and has come to be admired as the boldest innovator and perhaps the greatest poet in the literary history of the United States. This chapter gives a brief narrative of this reception, which has been largely a long-term success story. Whitman's status remains high, with new studies and editions of his work appearing monthly and appreciation for his poetry growing worldwide.

The first fifty years, 1855–1905

The success story starts with Emerson's famous letter. When Whitman sent Emerson a copy of the 1855 *Leaves*, the New England sage replied in a letter that greeted Whitman "at the beginning of a great career" and praised the power and candor of the work. Emerson was no doubt flattered by his obvious influence on the book, especially clear in the Preface and in the first poem, which would become "Song of Myself" – works that would always represent the farthest reaches of Whitman's Transcendentalism. "It meets the demand I am always making of what seemed the sterile & stingy nature, as if too much handiwork or too much lymph in the temperament were making our western wits fat & mean," Emerson said of the book. Though not without a touch of ambivalence here and there that would develop more fully and clearly in Emerson's later comments on *Leaves*, the letter's overall praise cannot be dismissed.[1]

Emerson shared the book with his New England friends, who found it odd but fascinating. Henry David Thoreau and Bronson Alcott wrote about it in their letters and visited Whitman in New York, as did Emerson himself. Whitman paid a visit to Boston late in 1856 and met with Thoreau and Alcott at the home of Henry Wadsworth Longfellow. In what became a kind of formula for the Transcendentalists, expressing a cautious reservation but at the same time stressing the seemingly lawless power and mystical depth as well as the peculiarly American quality of Whitman's poetry, Thoreau said in an 1856 letter, "Though rude and sometimes ineffectual, [*Leaves of Grass*] is a great primitive poem, – an alarum or trumpet-note ringing through the American camp. Wonderfully like the Orientals, too."[2]

The measured but generally warm reception Whitman enjoyed among Emerson's circle was certainly better than that in the many public reviews of his work. The most negative of these attacked Whitman's personal morality, his ideas, and his art. They accused Whitman of "licentiousness" and moral irresponsibility. They ridiculed his thought as the "disjointed babbling" of "some escaped lunatic, raving in pitiable delirium." They dismissed his effort to create new forms of poetry as "carelessness," "impertinence," "nonchalance with regard to forms," and "indifference to the dignity of verse." Even critics inclined to admire the vitality of the work hesitated as to its value as art. Charles A. Dana said that *Leaves of Grass* "cannot be especially commended either for fragrance or form," though "the taste of not overdainty fastidiousness will discern much of the essential spirit of poetry beneath an uncouth and grotesque embodiment." Another relatively appreciative critic of the 1855 edition, Charles Eliot Norton, described the poetry as "neither in rhyme nor blank verse, but in a sort of excited prose broken into lines without any attempt at measure or regularity, and without . . . any idea of sense or reason." Overall, the performance seemed to Norton "a mixture of Yankee transcendentalism and New York rowdyism." The same themes continued to be sounded in later reviews. Though he eventually came to regret the remarks, a young Henry James called *Drum-Taps* "an offense against art" and advised Whitman to reach beyond his personal and prophetic purposes to achieve the distance necessary to great literature.[3]

In the years before the Civil War, praise for Whitman's work was rarely unmixed. Even Emerson's response was more ambivalent than his 1855 letter may have suggested. Echoing Norton, his fellow New Englander, Emerson joked that *Leaves of Grass* mingled the *Bhagavad Gita* with the New York *Tribune*. When Whitman was preparing the 1860 edition, Emerson met with him in Boston and, according to Whitman's account, advised him to remove the "Enfans d'Adam" poems for the sake of both morality and marketability. Whitman's admirers among the bohemian circle in New York may have shared the Transcendentalists' ambivalence. The editor of the New York *Saturday Press*, Henry Clapp, published some of Whitman's best work, including the first version of "Out of the Cradle Endlessly Rocking," as well as a number of favorable reviews. But he also printed parodies of Whitman's work and applied his own famous wit to the oddities of Whitman's thought. "Walt, you include everything," Clapp is reputed to have quipped, "What do you have to say to the bed-bug?"[4] And despite his liberated sensibilities, Clapp seems to have more or less agreed with Emerson about "Children of Adam." A poet-prophet inclined to court readers as disciplines and "élèves" could only have felt disappointed at the halfway acceptance and jokes of the literati. He may even have had Clapp and the bohemians in mind when, in the postwar prose of *Democratic Vistas*, he complained about the "flippancy" of American intellectuals, their "tepid amours, weak infidelism, small aims, or no aims at all, only to kill time" (937).

Regardless of any discouragement he may have felt, however, Whitman called upon his journalistic savvy to make the most of the negative press. In addition to placing his own anonymous positive reviews in friendly papers, he also republished all the reviews, including the negative ones, in an appendix to *Leaves of Grass*. As a former newspaper editor, he knew that criticism and controversy sparked interest that could lead to sales and bring new readers who might take up the book out of curiosity and then become converts to the cause.

During his wartime years in Washington, the tide began to turn in his favor as Whitman discovered the kind of admiring readership his poems seem to demand, including the author of the first book on Whitman, the naturalist John Burroughs, and the poet's ardent defender, William Douglas O'Connor. O'Connor's 1866 pamphlet *The Good Gray Poet* uses the occasion of Whitman's dismissal from government office, allegedly because he had written an immoral book, to argue that the poet was in fact morally superior to most writers of the day – in his writing and in his actions, such as his work as a volunteer in the war hospitals. O'Connor, who saw Whitman as a literary genius on a par with Shakespeare and Milton, stresses the universality of the poetry, including the treatment of sex and the body, a topic that works of genius must necessarily confront if they are to account fully for human exuberance. By contrast, Burroughs' 1867 *Notes on Walt Whitman as Poet and Person* focuses on Whitman's special distinction among poets. He differs from nature poets like Wordsworth and Emerson, for example, because, according to Burroughs, he does not write *about* nature so much as he embodies it in his poetry and person. Likewise, he does not write *about* democracy so much as he brings it to life in written form. The argument from distinction seemed to appeal more to Whitman than the argument for the special status of the genius. Indeed Whitman contributed directly to the writing of Burroughs' *Notes*. Taken together, however, *The Good Gray Poet* and Burroughs' *Notes* covered all the angles in Whitman's defense.

With the help of his New England and Washington connections, Whitman made contact with admirers in England in the 1860s, including William Michael Rossetti, the brother of the poets Dante Gabriel Rossetti and Christina Rossetti, and a member of the famed Pre-Raphaelite circle that included such well-known and controversial intellectuals as the poet Algernon Charles Swinburne (whose mixed and sometimes reluctant admiration of Whitman was something like an edgy version of the Transcendentalist formula). William Rossetti was a critic and editor who created for the American poet an avenue to an international audience that has remained strong ever since. After much transatlantic deliberation and some consternation, Whitman agreed to allow Rossetti to bring out an edition of his poems, not *Leaves of Grass* as a whole, but a selection that would omit many of the problematic "poems of the body." For the rest of his life, the poet wavered over the wisdom of this decision, alternating between regret over what he viewed as a form of censorship on the one hand and, on the other, deep gratitude for the many appreciative readers who first encountered his poetry through Rossetti's edition.

In fact, the 1868 *Poems of Walt Whitman* did more than improve the poet's market status; it also took the critical study of *Leaves of Grass* to a new level. Rossetti's "Prefatory Notice" shows that the English critic wisely saw the opportunity to turn the critical debate away from issues of obscenity and the character of the author. Among other things, Rossetti insisted on a careful assessment of Whitman's poetic language. While admitting that some of the omitted passages were simply too raw for the English reading public, he did not apologize for the overall quality of the language, but rather praised the majesty and power of the work and was among the first to recognize Whitman's peculiar sensitivity to rhythm, movement, and cohesion even in the absence of rhyme and regular meter. Rossetti and his fellow Pre-Raphaelites were among the first critical readers to appreciate Whitman's iconoclastic refusal to conform to the conventions of the English poetic tradition. By somewhat artificially dividing the questions of morality from the questions of artfulness, Rossetti was thus able to sidestep the dismissal of Whitman's accomplishment on moral grounds and meet head-on the argument that Whitman was not a poet at all, an argument that was being advanced on both sides of the Atlantic.

Two important British readers who found their way to Whitman first through Rossetti's edition – and found their lives changed by the encounter – were Anne Gilchrist and Edward Carpenter. The widow of Blake's biographer who continued her husband's literary scholarship after his death, Gilchrist has been treated until recently with pity and condescension by Whitman scholars because of her transatlantic proposal of marriage to Whitman – the result of what proved a too-literal reading of the passionate persona in *Leaves of Grass*. This minor footnote

in the Whitman biography for many years unfairly overshadowed the importance of Gilchrist's essay "An English Woman's Estimate of Walt Whitman,"
the analytical brilliance of which is now widely recognized. A pioneering work
in gender-sensitive criticism, the essay is also remarkable for the unqualified
vigor of its acceptance of the whole of Whitman's project. Here we find no
disclaimers about the rawness or rudeness of the verse form or the question-
able morality of the poems on sex and the body. Ironic in light of the general
tendency of the Victorian male to "protect" the presumed sensitivity of women
readers, Gilchrist's "estimate" of *Leaves of Grass* joins those of O'Connor and
Burroughs in a complete acceptance of Whitman on his own terms.

Edward Carpenter, who was to become a major figure in the history of
homosexuality, discovered in Whitman a life-altering inspiration that enabled
him to find his own voice as a writer and social reformer. Carpenter was one
of a number of middle-class English readers who found in Whitman a source
of encouragement and a model for breaking free of stifling social and literary
conventions. Like the writer and social critic, John Addington Symonds, who
infamously questioned Whitman about his specific intentions in the "Calamus"
poems during the time he was writing a study of Whitman's poems in light
of its "Greek spirit," Carpenter responded to Whitman's call for a new form
of democracy based not on abstract principles but on the "love of comrades."
Carpenter's book-long poem *Towards Democracy* was an attempt to render
Whitman's ideas in language more accessible to a broad audience of middle-
class English readers. Like James William Wallace and John Johnston in their
"Bolton College" of Whitman enthusiasts, Carpenter (who was educated as a
clergyman but never practiced) also saw in *Leaves of Grass* the outlines of an
alternate religion, a kind of Whitmanism that linked close comradeship with
a kind of individual mystical experience, the direct perception of the power of
the divine in nature and human society. Like a number of Whitman followers
from the nineteenth century down to the present time, Carpenter linked his
sympathy for the power of *Leaves of Grass* with his own experience of mystical
wholeness.

Another exponent of the mystical reading was Richard Maurice Bucke, the
Canadian psychiatrist who became Whitman's friend, first biographer, and
one of his literary executors. As with Burroughs' 1867 book, Whitman wrote
extensive passages for Bucke's 1883 book *Walt Whitman* and made a number
of revisions in the manuscript. The ever democratic Whitman was above all
disconcerted by Bucke's view that he (Whitman) possessed an exalted moral
nature that put him on a par with the Buddha and Jesus Christ. For Bucke,
Section 5 of "Song of Myself" is a testimony to mystical illumination, to which
the remainder of Whitman's works and life bear substantial witness. While this

view was tempered by Whitman's editing of the 1883 book, it goes unfettered in Bucke's other books, *Man's Moral Nature* (1879) and *Cosmic Consciousness* (1901). The latter, a "New Age" classic still in print over one hundred years after its publication, proved popular and influential in religious studies. It is mentioned prominently, for example, in William James's *Varieties of Religious Experience*. While academic scholarship has often scoffed at Bucke's hagiographical treatment of Whitman, the mystical interest that he fostered retains an appeal for general audiences and has been followed by some interesting professional scholarship as well, including such provocative books as V. K. Chari's 1964 *Whitman in the Light of Vedantic Mysticism*, Lewis Hyde's 1979 *The Gift: Imagination and the Erotic Life of Property*, and George Hutchinson's 1986 *The Ecstatic Whitman: Literary Shamanism and the Crisis of the Union*. With their interest in restoring Whitman's mysticism to a social and historical context and respecting above all his democratic politics, the studies of Hyde and Hutchinson perhaps owe more to the tradition of the socialist Carpenter than that of Bucke with his insistence on placing Whitman in a special class of illuminati.

Another turn-of-the-century follower of Whitman who attempted to reconcile the mystical and political elements of Whitmanism was Horace Traubel, the poet's late-life companion and also a literary executor. Traubel visited the aging poet almost every day in the last four years of his life in Camden, New Jersey. Beginning in the early years of the twentieth century, he began publishing a multivolume treasure trove of the poet's sayings and conversations under the title *With Walt Whitman in Camden* (1906–96). While seemingly a self-effacing recorder of Whitman's talk, Traubel was able on many occasions subtly to turn the conversation toward his own interests, especially homosexuality and politics. Like Carpenter, Traubel was a socialist and champion of the working class. In later years, he became an activist in the US labor movement. He also developed an interest in Whitmanian mysticism (and provided testimony in Bucke's *Cosmic Consciousness*). But Traubel's major contribution to the critical reception of Whitman stemmed from his fastidiousness as a collector, preservationist, and promoter of Whitman's reputation among readers of all kinds. After the poet's death, he published a magazine *The Conservator*, dedicated almost exclusively to articles about Whitman.[5]

1905–1955

Professionalism and specialization set the tone for Whitman studies in the first half of the twentieth century. Academic scholars came to treat Whitman's early followers dismissively because of their seemingly uncritical adoration of the poet – that is, their lack of objectivity – and their willingness to make a religion of reading Whitman. As the prevailing attitude of professional criticism grew more skeptical and "scientific," the phrase from Bliss Perry's 1906 biography, "hot little prophets," haunted the scholarly perception of the earlier admirers and defenders.[6]

Perry himself, while not denying the spiritual elements in Whitman's work, was more inclined to psychologism in understanding sexual passion as the motivating force behind *Leaves of Grass* rather than sudden inspiration. He saw Whitman's development as an explainable process rather than a sudden miracle and was closely attentive to the work of the poet's literary apprenticeship. He also tended to replicate the Transcendentalists' judgments of Whitman as a lyrical genius but confused thinker who suffered from emotional excess – an ambivalence also repeated in assessments by many of the leading American poets of the day, such as Eliot and Pound. Ironically, Perry's cautious and critical attitude did not prevent him from swallowing the romantic fiction about a mysterious woman in New Orleans.

The story of Whitman's heterosexual romance, concocted by another early twentieth-century biographer, the Englishman Henry Bryan Binns in 1905, proved almost as durable as the dismissive attitude toward the early "Whitmaniacs." It would be repeated as late as 1971 when an old essay by William Carlos Williams was reprinted as the introduction to the *Illustrated Leaves of Grass*. The dream of aligning Whitman with a heterosexual norm informed (and virtually obsessed) the best candidate for the first true specialist in modern Whitman studies, the editor and biographer Emory Holloway. His 1926 book *Walt Whitman: An Interpretation in Narrative* won the Pulitzer Prize and served for the next thirty years as the definitive biography. Unfortunately, Holloway is remembered today primarily for his persistent belief that the poet had an affair and fathered children even when no good evidence appeared and when all signs pointed to Whitman's homoerotic preference. It was Holloway, in fact, who discovered the manuscript in which Whitman altered the genders of the pronouns in "Once I Pass'd Through a Populous City" (see Chapter 3).

Most critics who adhered to the emerging medical model of modern psychology were inclined to go in the opposite direction of Perry and Holloway and argue for a diagnosis of homosexuality, which was frequently treated as a pathology in the first half of the century. Thus began the dispute over the question of the poet's "nature" and the true character of his sexuality. It has never been fully resolved so much as it has dissolved in the rise of queer studies and the consensus of academic scholarship to accept the sexual ambivalence of *Leaves of Grass* as defiant of simplistic categories and reductive generalizations. Such an acceptance was impossible in the early years of sexology and psychoanalysis, however. The German critic Eduard Bertz, in the 1906 book ironically titled *Der Yankee-Heiland* (The Yankee Saint), argued that the reader trained in modern psychology could not fail to see a pathological feminine and hysterical quality in Whitman's poems, a pathology incompatible with the idea of Whitman's "sainthood." In the 1913 pamphlet *Walt Whitman's Anomaly*, W. C. Rivers likewise saw in Whitman's poems homosexuality of a passive and feminine type. Setting the stage for later, more sympathetic and critically sophisticated studies, Jean Catel applied the Freudian system to arrive at a different interpretation in his 1929 study *La naissance du poète*. Whitman was "born" as a poet, according to Catel, not when he realized his passion in a heterosexual or homosexual adventure, but rather when he accepted his own autoerotic nature and saw in his fantasies the kind of scenes and images that were the stuff of vision and poetry.

The professionalist trend in early twentieth-century scholarship overlapped with an ongoing polemic over Whitman's value as an artist. Among the defenders were Basil De Selincourt, an Englishman who offered a detailed analysis of Whitman's free-verse form in his 1914 *Walt Whitman: A Study*. Edward Carpenter, in his 1924 *Some Friends of Walt Whitman: A Study in Sex Psychology*, responded to the charges of psychopathology and called for an inquiry into the poet's sexuality that did not treat it as a crime or disease. William Sloane Kennedy, in his 1926 *The Fight of a Book for the World*, made the case for the success of *Leaves of Grass* by documenting the appreciation of a growing international audience. But the attack on *Leaves of Grass* continued. It took an interesting turn with the 1938 publication of Esther Shephard's *Walt Whitman's Pose*. Rather than lacking in artfulness, Shephard argued, Whitman was all too literary and was in fact hypocritical in foisting an image of himself as primitive and unschooled upon a naively receptive public at home and abroad. According to Shephard, both his book and his public persona were modeled on a character invented by the French novelist George Sand, whom the poet confessed to admiring. Whitman's claims to pure Americanism, great originality, authenticity, and confessional intimacy with the reader were, in Shephard's view, all a pathetic hoax.

Shephard's bitter attack was the exception rather than the rule by the 1930s, however. In addition to the number of modern writers who followed Whitman's path-breaking work in experimental form and free verse and who often acknowledged him,[7] the best sign of Whitman's general acceptance was the tendency of commentators and critics to abandon debate about the value of his work and pursue the study of his life and work within the contexts of literary and social history. Following the lead of the leftist Horace Traubel, Vernon Parrington in his 1927 *Main Currents in American Thought* and Newton Arvin in his

1938 *Whitman* stressed the revolutionary spirit and the materialist influence of science in *Leaves of Grass*, thus creating new avenues of appreciation for the poet of democracy in the age of the Great Depression. On the international scene, Whitman's reputation continued to spread with the appearance of such studies as the Danish critic Frederick Schyberg's 1933 *Walt Whitman*, which carefully treated the various editions of *Leaves of Grass* within their nineteenth-century American historical contexts but also regarded Whitman as a key figure of world literature, comparable in spirit and idea to Zola, Dostoevsky, and Nietzsche.

The study of vernacular literatures was itself little over a century old when the first doctoral dissertations on American literature began to appear in the 1920s. The emergence of the US as an international power in World War II, however, was accompanied on the academic front by increased interest in the specialized study of American literature. With the work of scholars like Emory Holloway and Harold Blodgett (whose 1934 book *Walt Whitman in England* was the first formal reception study of the poet), specialized study of Whitman's life and work came into its own.

The poet's status as a key figure in the new studies of American literature was settled once and for all by his inclusion in the highly influential 1941 book by F. O. Matthiessen, *American Renaissance: Art and Expression in the Age of Emerson and Whitman*. Matthiessen's work established the basic canon for American literature as emerging during the half-decade of 1850–55, which saw the publication of major works by Emerson, Thoreau, Hawthorne, Melville, and Whitman. These books deserve attention in modern times, Matthiessen argues, as works of art that fuse form and content in original ways to create a "living" text and a distinctive aesthetic experience for the reader. Matthiessen contends that Whitman's distinction from his contemporaries resides not only in his realization of the body rather than the personality or the psyche as a source of poetic power (inspiring formal as well as thematic innovation – the organic rhythms of his irregular, wave-like lines, for example) but also by his use of living forms of language that invigorate his poetic diction. According to Matthiessen, Whitman's experiment occasionally fails as the language descends into journalistic jargon – the Transcendentalist formula proving irresistible again. By noting the relation of Whitman's work to opera and painting, however, Matthiessen contends that despite occasional lapses in taste, *Leaves of Grass* stands firmly within the realm of the fine arts.

Matthiessen's aestheticism is complemented by the political and spiritual emphasis of another mid-century work in American literary scholarship, Henry Seidel Canby's 1943 critical biography *Walt Whitman: An American*. The America that Whitman celebrates, according to Canby, is not so much a real, historical entity as an ideal that incorporates the best of his fellow citizens' inner lives. In this view, the poet is prophetic in the deepest sense. He is certainly a close observer and critic of the contemporary scene, but his primary interest lies in what America could become by realizing its spiritual potential. Canby shares with the first generation of Whitman enthusiasts an appreciation of Whitman's technical innovations, spiritual motives, political energy, courage in challenging sexual mores, and open celebration of communal love. He differs in his modernist interest in psychology, in an inner life which he treats in a dialectical relation to nineteenth-century political history.

The trend toward specialization in Whitman studies is both realized and perpetuated in another book of this period, Gay Wilson Allen's 1946 *Walt Whitman Handbook*. This book served as a watershed of Whitman criticism up to mid-century – providing surveys of key influences on the poet, his philosophical foundations, his verse forms and main themes, and the current status of Whitman biography – and it pointed the way toward further work by specialists in biography, historical scholarship, textual scholarship, and formal criticism. Allen, who would update the handbook in *Walt Whitman: Man, Poet, and Legend* (1961) and *The New Walt Whitman Handbook* (1975), was destined to become the dean of Whitman studies in the second half of the twentieth century, taking critical biography to a new level and continuing to expand the study of Whitman's international reception.

1955–2005

By the one-hundredth anniversary of the first edition of *Leaves of Grass* in 1955, the dominant method of study in Anglo-American letters was the New Criticism, a formalist approach that favored close reading of the text as a self-contained, unique artifact; that disregarded political, psychological, and religious influences on and significances of the text; and that isolated the literary text from its biographical and historical contexts. At least in its purest manifestations, such a formalistic approach could only be antagonistic to a poet like Whitman whose life and works were inextricably linked to the rise of democracy in the New World and other events and movements on the historical scene, and whose book was taken by many readers as a guide to political and religious experience. Though Whitman studies eventually included some examples of text-based criticism that hovered close to the New Critical ideal, such as *A Critical Guide to Walt Whitman* (1957) by James E. Miller, Jr, and *Whitman: Explorations in Form* (1966) by Howard J. Waskow, Whitman was mainly ignored by the major New Critics in the US, such as Cleanth Brooks, Robert Penn Warren, Allen Tate, and John Crowe Ransom. A poet like Emily Dickinson, who spent most of her life confined to her father's house in a small New England town and who wrote tightly unified, self-reflexive, frequently ironic, and often riddling poems, fared much better among these critics (and thus required a greater effort by later biographers, historicists, and ideological critics to recover the latent political and sociological appeals of her work).

Contrary to what might be expected in such a critical environment, however, Whitman's reputation continued to flourish, partly because of his esteem in the American Studies movement, which emerged alongside the New Criticism in the postwar years of mid-century. Seemingly contrary to one another, New Criticism and American Studies were actually complementary. In treating literature primarily as a historical phenomenon among many related cultural artifacts, such as the visual arts, magazines, newspapers, and popular entertainment outlets, American Studies filled the niche vacated by the New Critics. At least in its early years, American Studies tended to avoid the detailed study of language and form, the kind of work formerly claimed by philology and then taken over by formalisms like the New Criticism.

Despite its inclination away from the kind of close reading that would seem to favor the study of poetry, however, American Studies could hardly ignore the poet of democracy. Whitman occupied a central place in such influential works as R. W. B. Lewis's *The American Adam: Innocence, Tragedy, and Tradition in the Nineteenth Century* (1955), which placed the poet firmly in the camp of "innocence" in developing the Adamic myth, and Roy Harvey Pearce's *The Continuity of American Poetry* (1961), which accepted Whitman as a prototype of the Adamic impulse and saw "Song of Myself" as a special version of American epic that favors the creativity of a new order of being over confirmation of an established order. With the commitment to contextualize Whitman's writing as fully as possible in its relationship to popular culture, the arts, the sciences, and various social movements, the American Studies movement continued to flourish throughout the 1980s and 1990s. Prominent examples include Harold Aspiz's study of the influence that nineteenth-century medical and health writings exerted on *Leaves of Grass* in *Walt Whitman and the Body Beautiful* (1980), David S. Reynolds' study of the relationship of low art to the high-art canon (including *Leaves of Grass*) in *Beneath the American Renaissance: The Subversive Imagination in the Age of Emerson and Melivlle* (1988), and the contextually attuned biographies of Justin Kaplan (*Walt Whitman: A Life*, 1980) and Reynolds (*Walt Whitman's America: A Cultural Biography*, 1995).

Almost as important to Whitman's advancing success as the American Studies movement was the willingness of biographical and historical critics to accommodate the methods of reading and language study associated with the

New Criticism. Nowhere is this accommodation clearer than in *The Solitary Singer* by Gay Wilson Allen, which was published on the anniversary of the first edition of *Leaves of Grass* in 1955 and served as the standard biography for several decades. It was at once the most detailed factual account of Whitman's life and the most New Critical of critical biographies in its approach to the poems. Allen treats Whitman as a self-contained loner, more of a modern individualist than a Romantic rebel. But overall his approach is more literary than psychological, sociological, or religious. Above all, Whitman was an artist who was able to rise above the sometimes sordid details of his personal life through the creation of a literary world in *Leaves of Grass*. Allen shares with aestheticists like Matthiessen and the New Critics (not to mention early critics like Henry James) a taste for distance and control, so that he is often as harshly critical of Whitman's emotional outpourings as he is admiring of Whitman's finest accomplishments. "Whitman's symbolical 'I,'" Allen writes, for example, "is usually esthetically successful," but "the impassioned confessions and out-cries of self-betrayal," though they may have some degree of "lyric power and beauty," overall "give the reader the impression that the poet vacillates between sublimity and pathos, between self-control and abandon, and consequent order and disorder in his esthetic form."[8]

Allen thus attempts a kind of tenuous resolution between biography and for-malist criticism. On the one hand, there is Whitman's historical existence, open to empirical research and inviting the biographer's narration of life processes – the birth, growth, and death of the poet himself and, by extension, the "life" of his book, its birth in 1855 and growth in successive editions. On the other hand, there is the world of the artist, which yields to the explications of the critic. Successful poems, in this view, originate in the life experiences, dreams, and fantasies of the biographical poet, but having been admitted into the realm of art, they lose their psychological significance and submit to the transforming effects of objective art. So far as they succeed, the poems are realizations of the laws that govern the realm of aesthetics. But if biographical motives and psycho-social-political agendas continue to intrude, the result can only be a failure of artistic integrity. Of course Allen also faced practical constraints. He was limited in the amount of close reading he could do and still sustain his biographical narrative. At best he could offer islands of explication within the general narrative flow and thus maintain a kind of tension between the story of Whitman's life in historical context and the reading of Whitman's poems under the aegis of New Critical values.

The analytical criticism of Richard Chase, whose *Walt Whitman Reconsidered* was also published in 1955, was not so constrained, though a similar tension prevailed in his need to reconcile close readings with a concern for historical and political contexts. Chase's work is important primarily because it stands almost exactly in the middle of what is considered, from the distance of several decades, the clear picture of New Critical formalism standing in forthright opposition to American Studies historicism. Very likely the two schools were never in complete opposition. Of the two works from the American Studies movement already mentioned, that of Roy Harvey Pearce definitely drew upon the close reading practices and themes of New Criticism. And the most New Critical of all Whitman scholars from this period, James E. Miller, Jr., frequently built his readings upon contextual awareness. Indeed, any critical theory is likely to become mixed in the actual work of practical criticism, especially when an individual author like Whitman is involved.

But Chase in particular was adamant in opposing the New Critical isolation of text from context, a method that, in his view, causes works of art to "wither before our eyes to the extent that we see them only as forms irreparably severed from the imperishable sources of being."[9] Formalist reading violates what is deepest and most meaningful in Whitman: the search for identity through the exploration of variety and diversity that greets the individual in the external world. Chase's genre criticism allows him both to treat the poems as expressions of the individual poet – "Whitman the comic poet, the radical realist, and the profound elegist" – and to delineate stages in the poet's career that correspond to movements in the historical context. The comic-epic (such as "Song of Myself") expresses "the large-mindedness, the complex versatility, the general vigor and adventurousness" as well as the "diversity" and "sexually versatile" perspectives of the prewar decades "which the war and the Gilded Age did much to destroy." The realist image poem captures the experience of the Civil War. And the elegy muses over the war's aftermath and mourns the loss of the early vigor and creative spirit.[10] Chase joins Allen in solidifying the dominant critical narrative of Whitman as losing his visionary inspiration after the war when his poems became more conventional. What's missing in these later performances is the tension – a concept whose value for Chase, along with his practice of close reading, aligns him with his opponents in the New Criticism. For Chase, the tension arises from historical as well as aesthetic factors. Whatever its source, without tension, poetry lacks life, in his view.

The biographical and historical methods of Allen and Chase, augmented by their close attention to the texts of the poems, and the view of Whitman as primarily a literary-historical figure (as opposed to the founder of a new religion or new system of thought) have remained the dominant approaches in academic Whitman studies ever since, though with a number of variations in emphasis. In the 1950s and 1960s, biographically inclined critics drifted even farther from the formalist pole of the critical spectrum by deepening their interest in the psychology of literary production. One strand of the psycholog-ical approach that goes back to the French critic Jean Catel – the treatment of sexuality as the chief source of personal creativity – was picked up in the fifties by another French scholar, the influential Whitman biographer and critic Roger Asselineau, who published *L'évolution de Walt Whitman* in 1954, the English version of which, *The Evolution of Walt Whitman: The Creation of a Personality*, first appeared in 1960. Whitman's literary art, Asselineau suggests, not only derived from aspects of his character but also deeply influenced the develop-ment of his personality over many years of practice. Thus rejecting the old Romantic tendency to judge Whitman on the basis of his sincerity, authentic-ity, or hypocrisy, Asselineau suggests that the great tension between art and life also comprises a dialectic of selfhood. Asselineau was also the first major critic to insist without compromise on the homosexuality of Whitman as a poet and person and to relate the development of his poetry to the inner struggle that he saw Whitman experiencing over the question of his sexuality. The realization of his attraction to other men in art became for Whitman at once the most painful and most important pursuit of his life.

Whereas Asselineau pulled back somewhat from the Freudian model of Catel, critics of the following decades displayed a deeper interest in psychoanalysis. They found Whitman and his poetry, especially the poems of 1855–60, a rich testing ground of dreamlike and sexually charged imagery in which to apply their theories. By far the most influential of the books to emerge from psy-choanalytical criticism was the 1968 *Walt Whitman's Poetry: A Psychological Journey* by Edwin Haviland Miller, a Whitman specialist who also edited six volumes of the poet's correspondence for the authoritative New York Univer-sity Edition of Whitman's works. The strength of Miller's book resides in his commitment to close readings developed within a mythic framework of the poet's career as a life journey. Extending Asselineau's concept of Whitman's life as a continual struggle marked by cyclic periods of growth and decline, Miller understands the evolution of *Leaves of Grass* as a courageous exploration of selfhood and search for emotional security. He suggests that more important than his literary background and apprenticeship, Whitman's troubled family life and unhappy childhood prompted his greatest poems as well as accounting for much of his adult behavior – his habit, for example, always to surround himself not only with literary admirers and intellectual equals but also with young men of the working classes, a kind of substitute band of brothers with whom he could construct the ideal family life denied him as a boy. In this light, Miller sees much of Whitman's political program as an overcompensating rant that intrudes upon the more authentic expression of the suffering self in the poems. Miller's readings of the poems – including especially strong treatments of "The Sleepers" and "Out of the Cradle Endlessly Rocking," the darkest of Whitman's performances in the early editions of *Leaves of Grass* – reveal the poetry's narcissistic and homosexual roots. While thus departing from the New Criticism with his interest in psychology and biography, Miller finds common ground with formalism in his penchant for close reading and his dismissive attitude toward politics. He is slightly more sympathetic to social and cultural readings that account for such factors as the Protestant attitude toward women and the isolation of the artist in a materialistic society. But the main work of psychoanalytical criticism, as practiced by Miller, is to weigh the stated purposes of the poet against the unconscious motives revealed in the symbols of the poems and the facts of the biography.

The psychoanalytic approach to Whitman studies has proved extremely productive. Following Miller, Stephen A. Black brought out *Whitman's Journey into Chaos* in 1975. The book offers an interesting view of the poet's compositional method as a kind of psychoanalytical deep-sea diving that brings unconscious materials to the surface of the mind to serve as the half-comprehended but energetic images and symbols of the poems. In the 1985 *My Soul and I: The Inner Life of Walt Whitman*, David Cavitch concentrates on images of the primal family as they emerge into the poetry from interior dialogues, a process that both produces the poems and stands as the primary content of the poems. This reading gives a psychoanalytic twist to a favorite idea of the New Criticism, that poetry, especially modern poetry, is always about poetry. Michael Moon's 1991 *Disseminating Whitman: Revision and Corporeality in Leaves of Grass* refreshes the psychoanalytic approach with Lacanian theory, body criticism, and deconstruction. Vivian Pollak's *The Erotic Whitman* of 2000 traces the anxiety associated with the development of a gendered identity throughout the evolution of *Leaves of Grass*. Daneen Wardrop in *Word, Birth, and Culture: The Poetry of Poe, Whitman, and Dickinson* and Beth Jensen in *Leaving the M/other: Whitman, Kristeva, and Leaves of Grass*, both published in 2002, introduce the poststructuralist psychoanalytical theory of Julia Kristeva into Whitman studies.

By the time of Moon, Pollak, Wardrop, and Jensen, in whose works appear the influences of queer theory and gender studies, psychoanalytical criticism was working harder to accommodate the influences of a revived historical and cultural criticism. Beginning in the late 1970s, critics had begun to reject the apolitical and clinical attitude of the earlier psychoanalytical school. What emerged was a new version of American cultural studies – sometimes aligned with the broader critical movement known as the New Historicism – that kept alive the interest in close reading from the New Criticism, the interest in sexuality and other elements of identity from psychoanalysis, and the interest in contextual influences from American Studies. The main thrust of this new work was a stronger emphasis on political ideology in Whitman's writing. Several concepts were imported from philosophical deconstruction and Marxist criticism, notably the idea that many elements of literature formerly thought to be under the control of the individual author or a property of the unified text were instead "socially constructed" properties of political ideology. The contexts of artistic production, in this view, are far more than mere background for the author's work. The context is as important as the author in determining the nature of the text. The degree to which the new studies subscribed to such views as the "death of the author" and the social constructedness of texts varied widely. But most would agree that, like any literary author, Whitman was an agent strongly influenced by social and political forces larger than himself and often beyond his control. And most would insist on the centrality of such key ideological issues as gender, class, and race.

At the forefront of these new studies was gay criticism, led by the pioneering work of Robert K. Martin. His 1979 survey *The Homosexual Tradition in American Poetry* portrays Whitman as the symbolic father of a long and deep legacy in modern American poetry. Martin shows how responsibility for the meaning of such works as the "Calamus" poems (which he contextualizes within such literary movements as the Platonic discourse on love and the nineteenth-century "friendship tradition") did not end with Whitman's "Deathbed Edition" but continue to be negotiated in the work of later gay writers, political activists, and literary critics. On the topic of class, M. Wynn Thomas in *The Lunar Light of Whitman's Poetry* (1987) builds upon new social histories to revise and specify Whitman's brand of democratic politics as the ideology of artisanal republicanism, which by Whitman's time was being overwhelmed by the rise of corporate capitalism. Race studies included such work as Martin Klammer's 1995 *Whitman, Slavery, and the Emergence of* Leaves of Grass, one of several studies to situate the struggle over slavery as the motive force behind Whitman's focus on freedom in his poetry. All of these social themes – and such others as imperialism and westward expansion – come together in Betsy Erkkila's *Whitman the Political Poet* (1989), which proved to be an influential point of convergence for ideological studies of Whitman from the 1970s and 1980s. Since then, political and historical criticism has continued to expand – promoting, for example, a revived interest in Whitman and the Civil War, a topic of focus in such studies as Robert Leigh Davis's 1997 *Whitman and the Romance of Medicine* and Jerome M. Loving's biography *Walt Whitman: The Song of Himself* (the factual updating of which makes this work the current standard in critical biography). More recently, the emergence of environmental politics on the world scene has inspired such studies as Lawrence Buell's 1995

The Environmental Imagination and 2001 *Writing for an Endangered World*, both of which include treatments of Whitman.

Despite enjoying a remarkable period of influence at the end of the twentieth century, structuralism, deconstruction, and poststructuralist criticism produced few inroads in Whitman studies. Even so, the effects of "high theory" have been felt. Besides the introduction of the concept of social construction and the ideological emphasis in New Historicism, another influence has been theory's "linguistic turn." In his 1983 book *Language and Style in* Leaves of Grass, C. Carroll Hollis applies semiotics and speech-act theory to new readings of Whitman's work, discovering (among other things) the particular usefulness of the concept of "performative" language in understanding Whitman's habit of directly addressing the reader and other elements of his style. James Perrin Warren extends this work in his 1990 *Walt Whitman's Language Experiment*, which situates Whitman's explicit and implicit theories of language within the history of linguistics and language philosophy. In *Walt Whitman and the American Idiom* (1991), Mark Bauerlein provides a deconstructionist echo of the favorite theme of New Criticism, that writing tends always to be about itself. Tenney Nathanson's 1992 *Whitman's Presence: Body, Voice, and Writing in* Leaves of Grass takes poststructuralism farther than any other specialized study of Whitman.

Like New Critical formalism, its distant cousin, however, deconstruction too often depends upon the notion of a closed self-referential text to have displaced the committed historicism of Whitman studies. Work in cultural studies, which currently predominates in Whitman criticism, nevertheless has taken the message that language matters and cannot be ignored in favor of macro-cultural issues such as race, class, and gender. Thus, in the frequently cited 1994 book *Walt Whitman's Native Representations*, Ed Folsom not only makes extensive use of close reading but also covers the topic of language directly in a major chapter on Whitman and the development of the American dictionary. And in the methodological introduction to a study of slavery, urbanization, and sexuality in the 1996 book *The Politics of Distinction: Whitman and the Discourses of Nineteenth-Century America*, Christopher Beach promotes the concept of "discourse" as a way of reuniting the study of culture and the study of language, which he feels have drifted apart in American literary criticism.

What becomes clear in the study of Whitman's reception in the various critical schools and in individual works of criticism is that nothing ever really goes away and that no school is ever completely eliminated by another but only overshadowed, to be revealed again (or reinvented) as time passes. Another certainty is that popular responses rarely follow the trends of academic fashion. Whitmanian mysticism, for example, once almost totally abandoned in the professionalization of criticism and the advent of cultural materialism, has continued to attract adherents and new readers throughout the world. What remains, then, is a complex layering of perspectives. With each new interpretation – not only in biography and criticism, but in all the poems, novels, paintings, photographs, and films, not to mention the political movements and social causes, on which Whitman has left his mark as an iconic American poet – the legacy of his work only grows richer and deeper.

Notes

1 Life

1. Walt Whitman, *Complete Poetry and Collected Prose* (Washington, DC: Library of America, 1982), p. 610. All further references throughout the book are given in parentheses.
2. Walt Whitman, *An American Primer*, Horace Traubel (ed.), (Stevens Point, WI: Holy Cow!, 1987), pp. viii–ix.
3. Quoted in Joann P. Krieg, *A Whitman Chronology* (Iowa City: University of Iowa Press, 1998), p. 10.
4. Horace Traubel, *With Walt Whitman in Camden* (New York: Rowman and Littlefield, 1961), vol. I, p. 93.
5. Jerome M. Loving, *Walt Whitman: The Song of Himself* (Berkeley, CA: University of California Press, 1999), p. 179.
6. Kenneth M. Price (ed.), *Walt Whitman: The Contemporary Reviews* (Cambridge: Cambridge University Press, 1996), pp. 8, 18, 23.
7. Quoted in Loving, *Walt Whitman*, p. 189.
8. Walt Whitman, *Notebooks and Unpublished Prose Manuscripts*, Edward F. Grier (ed.), (New York: New York University Press, 1984), vol. I, p. 353.
9. Quoted in Krieg, *Whitman Chronology*, p. 53.
10. Quoted in Loving, *Walt Whitman*, p. 274.
11. Walt Whitman, *Drum-Taps (1865) and Sequel to Drum-Taps (1865–66): A Facsimile Reproduction*, F. DeWolfe Miller (ed.), (Gainesville, FL: Scholars' Facsimiles and Reprints, 1959), p. xxix.
12. Whitman, *Notebooks*, vol. II, p. 539.
13. See Loving, *Walt Whitman*, p. 285, for an appropriately cautious view of the evidence.
14. Martin G. Murray, "'Pete the Great': A Biography of Peter Doyle," *Walt Whitman Quarterly Review* 12 (1994), 1–51.
15. Kenneth M. Price, *To Walt Whitman, America* (Chapel Hill: University of North Carolina Press, 2004), p. 1.

2 Historical and cultural contexts

1. See M. Wynn Thomas, *The Lunar Light of Whitman's Poetry* (Cambridge, MA: Harvard University Press, 1987); also Alan Trachtenberg, *The Incorporation of America: Culture and Society in the Gilded Age* (New York: Hill and Wang, 1982).
2. Jerome M. Loving, *Walt Whitman: The Song of Himself* (Berkeley: University of California Press, 1999), pp. 153–60.
3. Quoted in David S. Reynolds, *Walt Whitman's America: A Cultural Bibliography* (New York: Knopf, 1995), p. 119.
4. Sherry Ceniza, *Walt Whitman and 19th-Century Women Reformers* (Tuscaloosa: University of Alabama Press, 1998).
5. See Harold Azpiz, *Walt Whitman and the Body Beautiful* (Urbana: University of Illinois Press, 1980); and Reynolds, *Walt Whitman's America.*
6. William Blackstone, *Commentaries on the Laws of England,* John Frederick Archbold (ed.), (London: William Reed, 1811), vol. IV, p. 215.
7. Quoted in Milton Hindus (ed.), *Walt Whitman: The Critical Heritage* (New York: Barnes and Noble, 1971), p. 33.
8. Quoted in Horace Traubel, *With Walt Whitman in Camden* (New York: Mitchell Kennerley, 1914), vol. III, pp. 452–3.
9. Justin Kaplan, *Walt Whitman: A Life* (New York: Simon and Schuster, 1980), p. 107.
10. For a good overview of criticism, see Walter Grünzweig's essay "Imperialism" in *A Companion to Walt Whitman,* Donald D. Kummings (ed.), (Oxford: Blackwell, 2006), pp. 151–63. Grünzweig concludes that "Whitman's imperialism . . . is one which looks beyond, which implies, and indeed includes the forces and tools which will help overcome it" (p. 162).
11. See H. T. Kirby-Smith, *The Origins of Free Verse* (Ann Arbor, MI: University of Michigan Press, 1996).
12. Quoted in Loving, *Walt Whitman,* p. 226.
13. See "Images of Whitman" in the online *Walt Whitman Archive* and Ed Folsom's useful introduction, "Nineteenth-century Visual Culture" in *A Companion to Walt Whitman,* pp. 272–89.

3 Poetry before the Civil War

1. William James, *The Varieties of Religious Experience* (New York: Touchstone, 1997), pp. 82–85; Richard Maurice Bucke, *Walt Whitman* (Philadelphia: McKay, 1883) and *Cosmic Consciousness* (New York: Dutton, 1969).
2. This discussion, as well as that in the next paragraph, draws upon the fine summary in James Perrin Warren's entry on "Style and Technique(s)" in *Walt Whitman: An Encyclopedia,* J. R. LeMaster and Donald D. Kummings (eds.), (New York: Garland, 1998), pp. 693–6. See also Warren's *Walt Whitman's Language Experiment* (University Park: Pennsylvania State University Press, 1990).

3. Ralph Waldo Emerson, *Nature*, in *Essays and Lectures* (New York: Library of America, 1983), p. 10.

4. Ralph Waldo Emerson, "Self-Reliance," in *Essays and Lectures*, p. 265.

5. See Helen Vendler, *Poets Thinking: Pope, Whitman, Dickinson, Yeats* (Cambridge, MA: Harvard University Press, 2004).

6. Lawrence, "Whitman," in *Leaves of Grass: Norton Critical Edition*, Sculley Bradley and Harold W. Blodgett (eds.), (New York: Norton, 1973), p. 847.

7. Walt Whitman, "Live Oak, with Moss." *The Walt Whitman Archive*, Kenneth M. Price and Ed Folsom (ed.). http://www.whitmanarchive.org/.

8. Jerome M. Loving, *Walt Whitman: The Song of Himself* (Berkeley, CA: University of California Press, 1999), pp. 249–50.

4 Poetry after the Civil War

1. On sentimentality versus romanticism, see Ann Douglas, *The Feminization of American Culture* (New York: Knopf, 1977), p. 255; on sentimentality in Whitman, see M. Jimmie Killingsworth, *Whitman's Poetry of the Body: Sexuality, Politics, and the Text* (Chapel Hill: University of North Carolina Press, 1989), pp. 93–6.

2. Horace Traubel, *With Walt Whitman in Camden* (New York: Rowman and Littlefield, 1961), vol. II, p. 304.

3. See Jerome M. Loving, *Walt Whitman: The Song of Himself* (Berkeley, CA: University of California Press, 1999), p. 288.

4. See Mark Maslan's discussion of these issues in *Whitman Possessed: Poetry, Sexuality and Popular Authority* (Baltimore: Johns Hopkins University Press, 2001).

5. This shift in the general culture is nicely documented by Kenneth Cmiel in *Democratic Eloquence: The Fight over Popular Speech in America* (Berkeley: University of California Press, 1991); and Garry Wills, *Lincoln at Gettysburg: The Words that Remade America* (New York: Simon & Schuster, 1992).

6. Ezra Pound, "In a Station at the Metro," William Carlos Williams, "The Red Wheelbarrow," in Richard Ellmann (ed.), *The New Oxford Book of American Verse* (New York: Oxford University Press, 1976), pp. 502 and 469.

7. See the discussion of this poem with contributions by Ed Folsom in M. Jimmie Killingsworth, *Walt Whitman and the Earth: A Study in Ecopoetics* (Iowa City: University of Iowa Press, 2004).

8. Loving, *Walt Whitman*, p. 461.

5 Prose works

1. The difficulty of attribution is demonstrated strongly in Jerome M. Loving's recent critical biography *Walt Whitman: The Song of Himself* (Berkeley, CA: University of California Press, 1999).

2. The Emerson–Whitman relationship is the prototype in Harold Bloom's famous study, *The Anxiety of Influence: A Theory of Poetry* (New York: Oxford University Press, 1973).

3. For an extensive treatment of the importance of place in *Specimen Days* and in Whitman's work in general, see M. Jimmie Killingsworth, *Walt Whitman and the Earth: A Study in Ecopoetics* (Iowa City: University of Iowa Press, 2004).

4. Peter Coviello's recent edition of *Memoranda during the War* (New York: Oxford University Press, 2004) restores the original version along with an extensive introduction, which provides the best treatment of this work to date.

5. On the historical context of Whitman's treatment of the weather, see the excellent chapter in M. Wynn Thomas's recent book *Transatlantic Connections: Whitman US, Whitman UK* (Iowa City: University of Iowa Press, 2005).

6. See the outstanding treatment of the influence of photography in Whitman's later writings within the context of modernist poetry in Ed Folsom's *Walt Whitman's Native Representations* (Cambridge: Cambridge University Press, 1994).

6 Critical reception

1. Emerson's letter quoted in Jerome M. Loving, *Walt Whitman: The Song of Himself* (Berkeley: University of California Press, 1999), p. 189. On the letter's possible ambivalence, see Jay Grossman, *Reconstituting the American Renaissance: Emerson, Whitman, and the Politics of Representation* (Durham, NC: Duke University Press, 2003).

2. Quoted in Milton Hindus, ed., *Walt Whitman: The Critical Heritage* (New York: Barnes and Noble, 1971), p. 68.

3. The quotations in this paragraph are taken from the wealth of reviews available in the Criticism section of the online *Walt Whitman Archive*, edited by Kenneth M. Price and Ed Folsom.

4. Quoted in Albert Parry, *Garrets and Pretenders: A History of Bohemianism in America* (New York: Covici and Friedi, 1933), p. 39.

5. Much work remains to be done on Whitman's early critics and disciples. In recent scholarship Gary Schmidgall offers a good treatment of the Whitman–Traubel relationship in *Walt Whitman: A Gay Life* (New York: Dutton, 1997) and has also edited a selection of items from *With Walt Whitman in Camden* and another group of excerpts from *The Conservator* (both published by the University of Iowa Press). See also the chapter on Traubel in Bryan K. Garman's *A Race of Singers: Whitman's Working-Class Hero from Guthrie to Springsteen* (Chapel Hill: University of North Carolina Press, 2000).

6. It was actually Gay Wilson Allen who first applied the phrase "hot little prophets" to the early biographers in his influential essay on Whitman biography in the *Walt Whitman Handbook* (Chicago: Packard, 1946), p. 23. Perry used the epithet in an offensive remark about Whitman's imitators in free verse: "freaks and cranks and

neurotic women, with here and there a hot little prophet," in *Walt Whitman* (Boston: Houghton Mifflin, 1906), pp. 285–6. Only very recently have Whitman's disciples received serious consideration, in the work of Schmidgall (see note 4) and in work in progress by Michael Robertson and Steve Marsden.

7. The best introduction to and survey of the influence of Whitman upon appreciative (and sometimes ambivalent) modern literary artists is the outstanding collection, *Walt Whitman: The Measure of his Song*, 2nd edition, edited by Jim Perelman, Ed Folsom, and Dan Campion (Stevens Point, WI: Holy Cow! Press, 1999).

8. Gay Wilson Allen, *The Solitary Singer* (New York: Macmillan, 1955), pp. 161–2.

9. Richard Chase, *Walt Whitman Reconsidered* (New York: Sloane, 1955), p. 98.

10. Chase, *Walt Whitman Reconsidered*, pp. 8, 15, 27.

Further reading

Note: This list includes only books (no articles or chapters) and focuses on those that are still in print and readily available. Many older works are briefly mentioned in the discussion of the critical reception in Chapter 6 and in the chapter notes. The idea here is to offer a place for the serious student of Whitman to take the next step into the extensive literature on the poet and his work. Readers interested in further study should consult, in addition to the usual resources, the searchable bibliography available online in *The Walt Whitman Archive.*

Allen, Gay Wilson, and Folsom, Ed (eds), *Walt Whitman and the World.* Iowa City: University of Iowa Press, 1995. The best point of entry into the study of Whitman's international reputation, reception, and worldwide fame.

Aspiz, Harold, *So Long!: Walt Whitman's Poetry of Death.* Tuscaloosa: University of Alabama Press, 2004. The fullest treatment of Whitman's elegiac work and the most balanced consideration of the influence of Protestant Christianity upon the poet.

Bauerlein, Mark, *Whitman and the American Idiom.* Baton Rouge: Louisiana State University Press, 1991. A study informed by recent work in semiotics and poststructuralism that focuses on the language theories that Whitman explicitly encountered and entertained and those implicit in his poetry.

Beach, Christopher, *The Politics of Distinction: Whitman and the Discourses of Nineteenth-Century America.* Athens: University of Georgia Press, 1996. An attempt to unite the study of language and ideology in a critical look at race and slavery, urbanization, and the (sexual) body in Whitman's poetry and its historical context.

Burrows, Edwin G., and Wallace, Mike, *Gotham: A History of New York City to 1898.* New York: Oxford University Press, 1999. The most up-to-date general history of the geographical and political setting for Whitman's life and works.

Ceniza, Sherry, *Walt Whitman and 19th-Century Women Reformers.* Tuscaloosa: University of Alabama Press, 1998. A study of how women responded to Whitman's works in his own time, with a focus on specific women whom he influenced and who influenced him.

Davis, Robert Leigh, *Whitman and the Romance of Medicine.* Berkeley: University of California Press, 1997. A good treatment of how Whitman's experience in the Civil War hospitals influenced his poetry.

Erkkila, Betsy, *Whitman the Political Poet.* New York: Oxford University Press, 1989. The most complete introduction to the political contexts of Whitman's writing; good coverage of political movements in his own day as well as the implications of his writings for recent social and political movements involving race, class, gender, and other topics.

Erkkila, Betsy, and Grossman, Jay (eds.), *Breaking Bounds.* New York: Oxford University Press, 1996. A collection of essays by innovative scholars that sample newer critical approaches to Whitman, including cultural studies, queer studies, and feminism/gender studies.

Folsom, Ed, *Walt Whitman's Native Representations.* Cambridge: Cambridge University Press, 1994. A study of Whitman's relation to four areas of cultural interest: language, Native Americans, photography, and baseball.

Folsom, Ed (ed.), *Whitman East and West: New Contexts for Reading Walt Whitman.* Iowa City: University of Iowa Press, 2002. A collection of recent essays on Whitman with an emphasis on historical, political, and international connections, both Asian and European.

Fone, Byrne R. S., *Masculine Landscapes: Walt Whitman and the Homoerotic Text.* Carbondale: Southern Illinois University Press, 1992. Perhaps the most textually thorough book focusing on the treatment of same-sex love in Whitman's poetry.

Greenspan, Ezra, *Walt Whitman and the American Reader.* Cambridge: Cambridge University Press, 1990. Whitman's poetry in the context of book history and nineteenth-century literary culture, including such topics as publication trends and reading practices.

Grossman, Jay, *Reconstituting the American Renaissance: Emerson, Whitman, and the Politics of Representation.* Durham: Duke University Press, 2003. A provocative reconsideration of the relationship of Whitman and Emerson in the context of constitutional issues in American political history and other topics (notably social class and attitudes toward the body).

Grünzweig, Walter, *Constructing the German Walt Whitman.* Iowa City: University of Iowa Press, 1995. An extensive study of Whitman's reception in Germany and in German literature.

Killingsworth, M. Jimmie, *Walt Whitman and the Earth: A Study in Ecopoetics.* Iowa City: University of Iowa Press, 2004. A study of Whitman's nature writing in light of recent developments in ecocriticism and the history of environmentalism since Whitman's time.

Killingsworth, M. Jimmie, *Whitman's Poetry of the Body: Sexuality, Politics, and the Text.* Chapel Hill: University of North Carolina Press, 1989. A non-biographical treatment of hetero- and homoeroticism in Whitman's poetry in the context of the history of sexuality and sexual politics.

Klammer, Martin, *Whitman, Slavery, and the Emergence of* Leaves of Grass. University Park: Pennsylvania State University Press, 1995. A treatment of the importance of slavery as a topic in the poetry and a context for the genesis of such key poems as "Song of Myself."

Krieg, Joann, *Walt Whitman and the Irish*. Iowa City: University of Iowa Press, 2000. A study of Whitman's attitudes toward the Irish during the period of heavy immigration in nineteenth-century America as well as Whitman's reception in Ireland.

Krieg, Joann, *A Whitman Chronology*. Iowa City: University of Iowa Press, 1998. A highly useful sketch of Whitman's life and times, including key events in the historical context and publication dates; brief but substantive notes amount to a biography in miniature.

Kummings, Donald D. (ed.), *A Companion to Walt Whitman*. Oxford: Blackwell, 2006. A collection of overviews of key themes and texts in Whitman's work by major scholars, particularly strong on cultural and political contexts.

Larson, Kerry, *Whitman's Drama of Consensus*. Chicago: University of Chicago Press: 1988. Close readings of Whitman's major poems deeply informed by ideology, language study, and literary theory, with an emphasis on the inconclusive interplay of diverse political perspectives.

LeMaster, J. R., and Kummings, Donald D. (eds.), *Walt Whitman: An Encyclopedia*. New York: Garland, 1998. An extensive and authoritative resource that provides entries on most of the individual writings and genres of Whitman's work, as well as key themes, historical topics, people, and places associated with Whitman.

Loving, Jerome M., *Emerson, Whitman, and the American Muse*. Chapel Hill: University of North Carolina Press, 1982. Discusses Whitman in the context of Transcendentalism and the American Romantic movement.

Loving, Jerome M., *Walt Whitman: The Song of Himself*. Berkeley: University of California Press, 1999. Currently the standard critical biography of Whitman, with a particularly good treatment of the centrality of the Civil War in Whitman's life and works.

Mack, Stephen, *The Pragmatic Whitman*. Iowa City: University of Iowa Press, 2002. An important philosophical study that traces Whitman's lineage of democratic thought through the evolution of American pragmatism, particularly the secular and empirical tradition of John Dewey.

Maslan, Mark, *Whitman Possessed: Poetry, Sexuality and Popular Authority*. Baltimore: Johns Hopkins University Press, 2001. A critical and literary-historical examination of Whitman's poetics of inspiration, ideology, and desire through the trope of demonic possession.

Miller, Edwin Haviland, *Walt Whitman's "Song of Myself": A Mosaic of Interpretations*. Iowa City: University of Iowa Press, 1989. A collection of various critical readings of Whitman's most famous poem, arranged line by line with additional commentary by the distinguished psychoanalytical critic and editor of Whitman's letters.

Moon, Michael, *Disseminating Whitman: Revision and Corporeality in* Leaves of Grass. Cambridge, MA: Harvard University Press, 1991. The body and sexuality in light of poststructuralist criticism and particularly Lacanian psychoanalysis.

Morris, Roy, Jr., *The Better Angel: Walt Whitman in the Civil War*. New York: Oxford University Press, 2000. A brief and highly readable narrative of Whitman's experiences in the Civil War with commentary on the effects of the war on his career as a poet.

Nathanson, Tenney, *Whitman's Presence: Body, Voice, and Writing in* Leaves of Grass. New York: New York University Press, 1992. Whitman's poetry as an example of the problem of presence as conceived by deconstructive criticism.

Perelman, Jim, Folsom, Ed, and Campion, Dan, *Walt Whitman: The Measure of His Song*, 2nd edition. Stevens Point, WI: Holy Cow! Press, 1999. An extensive collection of modern poets and writers from around the world who comment on Whitman's influence and impact on their work.

Pollak, Vivian, *The Erotic Whitman*. Berkeley: University of California Press, 2000. A primarily psychoanalytical approach to the anxiety of gender implicit in Whitman's poetry of the body.

Price, Kenneth M., *Whitman and Tradition: The Poet in His Century*. New Haven, CT: Yale University Press, 1990. Whitman in the context of Anglo-American literary history.

Price, Kenneth M., *To Walt Whitman, America*. Chapel Hill: University of North Carolina Press, 2004. Whitman iconography and influence in twentieth-century American culture, including social movements (involving race, sexuality, and gender, for example), literature, and film.

Reynolds, David S., *Walt Whitman's America: A Cultural Biography*. New York: Knopf, 1995. The fullest treatment of Whitman's life and work in the context of nineteenth-century social issues, popular culture, politics, and art.

Reynolds, David S. (ed.), *A Historical Guide to Walt Whitman*. New York: Oxford University Press, 2000. Includes a short biography as well as chapters on race, sexuality, democratic politics, and visual arts.

Selby, Nick, *The Poetry of Walt Whitman*. New York: Palgrave Macmillan, 2004. An overview of Whitman criticism (snippets of sample works in the history of the critical reception and commentary by Selby) with a special slant toward ideological criticism, including the later work of Karen Sanchez-Eppler and Jonathan Arac.

Thomas, M. Wynn, *The Lunar Light of Whitman's Poetry*. Cambridge, MA: Harvard University Press, 1987. A study of Whitman's poetry keyed to the development of his political thinking and the ideology of artisanal republicanism.

Thomas, M. Wynn, *Transatlantic Connections: Whitman US, Whitman UK*. Iowa City: University of Iowa Press, 2005. Further thoughts on the historical and political contexts of Whitman's work as well as studies of the poet's British reception.

Wardrop, Daneen, *Word, Birth, and Culture: The Poetry of Poe, Whitman, and Dickinson*. Westport, CT: Greenwood, 2002. Homosexuality and the limits of linguistic experience in Whitman as one of three poets who made marginalized sexual choices in the context of nineteenth-century culture.

Warren, James Perrin, *Walt Whitman's Language Experiment.* University Park: Pennsylvania State University Press, 1990. A study of the language and style of Whitman's writings in light of nineteenth- and twentieth-century theories of language.

Whitman, Walt, *Complete Poetry and Collected Prose.* New York: Library of America, 1982. The most complete and reliable single-volume collection of the poet's work (selected by Justin Kaplan); includes only minimal critical apparatus (no introduction or footnotes, for example).

Whitman, Walt, *The Walt Whitman Archive*, Kenneth M. Price and Ed Folsom (eds.). http://www.whitmanarchive.org/. An indispensable online resource with complete editions of Whitman's work as well as searchable bibliography, manuscript reproductions, and other scholarly aids.

Index